Grapes Of Wrath
Or Grace?

Grapes Of Wrath Or Grace?

Sermons For Pentecost
(First Third)
Cycle C First Lesson Texts

Barbara Brokhoff

CSS Publishing Company, Inc.
Lima, Ohio

GRAPES OF WRATH OR GRACE?

Reprinted in 2003

Copyright © 1994 by
CSS Publishing Company, Inc.
Lima, Ohio

Library of Congress Cataloging-in-Publication Data

Brokhoff, Barbara.
     Grapes of wrath or grace? : sermons for Pentecost (first third) first lesson, cycle C /
Barbara Brokhoff.
         p.   cm.
     ISBN 0-7880-0035-7
     1. Pentecost season—Sermons. 2. Bible. N. T. Gospels—Sermons. 3. Sermons, American. I. Title.
     BV4300.5.B767   1994
     252'.6—dc20   94-1002
                                                                                  CIP

For more information about CSS Publishing Company resources, visit our website at www.csspub.com or e-mail us at custserv@csspub.com or call (800) 241-4056.

This book is available in the following formats, listed by ISBN:
0-7880-0035-7 Book
0-7880-0036-5 Disk
0-7880-0037-3 Book and Disk package

PRINTED IN U.S.A.

This book is dedicated, with love, to R.C., the Res-Theo of North Carolina and who is also A.A.A, A.A.R., and best of all, a Lover of Christ.

— Barbara Brokhoff

Table Of Contents

C — Revised Common Lectionary; L — Lutheran Lectionary; RC — Roman Catholic Lectionary

The
All-Occasion Wine

My brother, B.J., is a connoisseur of fine wine and, as such, can tell you what a good wine tastes like, what properties and bouquets to look for, and how it is to be used. Of course tastes in wine very widely, but he suggests a full-bodied red wine with red meat and a lighter, dryer wine with fish and chicken. He would recommend a sweeter wine, perhaps port or brandy, for after dinner. For Lutherans, Episcopalians, Catholics, and others there is always what is known as "Communion Wine," and for United Methodists there is simple Welch's grape juice (which really isn't wine at all). It has been said that the difference between a Lutheran and a United Methodist is that a Lutheran uses real wine and a United Methodist uses real bread.

It must not be forgotten that some write all wines off as bad, evil, sinful, and a product of the devil. There is no question that wine can be terribly misused and then becomes a curse.

On the Day of Pentecost, when the Holy Spirit fell upon the waiting disciples, there were a number of extraordinary events occurring: there was the sound of a rushing wind, cloven tongues of fire appeared, and they all began to speak in other languages and the Holy Spirit gave them ability. The Jews who were visiting Jerusalem, from all nations, hearing them speak in their own tongues, were amazed at this startling phenomenon. They came to the hasty, false conclusion that the disciples must be drunk, and accused them, saying, "They have had too much wine!" "Not so!" said Peter. "It is only nine in the morning — far too early to be foxed. They are not drunk, but rather filled with the new wine of the Spirit. This is what Joel the prophet foretold many years ago."

In other words, the Holy Spirit is *New Wine* and it cannot make you drunk. The Spirit will not cloud your mind, it won't cause you to talk stupidly, it won't make you an unsafe driver, and it won't give you a hangover. The disciples were not inebriated, but rather filled with God the Holy Spirit. They had not imbibed on the fruit of the vine, nor had they drunk the nectar of the gods, but they had been filled with the Divine Nectar, the New Wine from heaven. This Spirit will be a wine for all occasions, for all people.

Before his Ascension, Jesus had wanted his followers to know that the same Lord who had called them and ministered to them in his physical presence would now, through the Holy Spirit, *always* be with them. They must realize that the crucified, resurrected, and now ascended Lord would return. The same Spirit which dwelt in him would now dwell in them.

On this anniversary of the Day of Pentecost, when the Christian Church was born, let us be deeply grateful that the Spirit of Christ, in the power of the Holy Spirit, has come to us. Without the Holy Spirit, Christian discipleship would be impossible. We would have no understanding of spiritual things without the Spirit of Truth. We would never enjoy Christian fellowship with one another without the unity of the Spirit. We could never be effective Christian witnesses without the Spirit's power. In fact, we would have no life without the life-giving Spirit. Just as the body without breath is a corpse, so a church without the Holy Spirit is dead!

Since the Holy Spirit's presence in our midst is so essential for our very existence, we should long for the Holy Spirit, pray for the Holy Spirit, and open ourselves to his coming. What do you suppose would happen to us as individual Christians, and as a church, if we would adopt the same formula to ready ourselves for the Spirit as did those early disciples in the upper room? Would Pentecost re-occur in us?

They Waited And Prayed

The disciples met in the upper room, and for ten days they tarried — they waited and prayed for the promise of the Father. Jesus wanted his disciples to be people who would not rush in headlong on their own, independent of God's guidance. He wanted them to wait for God. What an impossible task that must have seemed to those early believers. Christ was alive and they wanted to act. Jesus said "wait" and they wanted to "move."

"Wait" is a cruel word for our frenetic, frenzied, whirling, busy selves, too. We are so impetuous and impatient. Why write it when you can phone or fax it? We expect instant results and instant action. After all, we have instant foods and instant drinks, so why not instant results and instant responses? We can't wait. We want people to understand now! We want people to change now! Waiting for the Lord's leading and timing is so hard, but still Jesus said to do it: "Wait for the promised Holy Spirit." Don't run ahead of God, for if you run without waiting on God, you will run with no power (and with disastrous results). If you try to "hurry up" the hatching of a baby bird or chick, you only destroy the baby to be born. So, too, when we run ahead of God do we destroy the wonderful plan that he has in mind.

So, having been told to "tarry," the disciples went to that upper chamber to wait and to pray. In fact, they devoted themselves to prayer. What must it have been like as they met in that room for the first two or three days? They would be gathered in close physical proximity, but their wills might well have been miles apart. The confinement would lend itself to arguments and dissension. Remember, these were normal people like you and me. There had been a lot of disagreements among them previously. They had experienced sharp divisions over rank, importance, and who would have the highest seat. They were strong-willed persons with conflicting ideas. But the waiting and the praying began to do something for them, for the scripture says that they (on the tenth day of waiting),

11

when the Spirit came, were of *one* accord! Imagine that! As they prayed and tarried they became fully open to God and more loving toward each other. Such harmony and peace prepared their hearts to receive the Holy Spirit.

A man tells of being on a bus tour in Rome which was led by a guide who spoke English. Their first stop was a basilica in a piazza which was surrounded by several lanes of relentless Roman traffic. After they were all safely dropped off, the group climbed the steps for a quick tour of the church. Then they spread out to board the bus, which was parked across the street from the church. The frantic guide shouted for the group to stay together. He hollered out to them, "You cross one by one, they hit you one by one. But if you cross together, they think you will hurt the car!" There is always much to be said for unity, particularly the unity of the Spirit.

Contentious people cannot receive the Spirit's presence. If, as individuals, and as a church, we desire the Holy Spirit, it might be well to ask ourselves: "Am I in unity with God? Is everyone forgiven? Has restitution been made? Am I holding a grudge? Am I in love and harmony with God and neighbor?" Until we are of one mind and heart, until we love each other as Christ loved us, until all broken relationships are healed, the power of Pentecost cannot come to us!

Note The Specifics Of The Spirit's Coming

It is rather remarkable at how specific the scriptures are concerning the events of the Day of Pentecost. We know a lot of the particulars about this astounding Gift from heaven. Have you ever noticed that everything that is precious to you is related to time, persons, and place? For instance, I shall never forget the first time I met my husband John. It was August. It was at a pastors' school, on the campus of Central College in Fayette, Missouri. I recall that he wore a black suit, a black shirt, and a white clerical collar. I first thought he might be a Catholic priest or an Episcopalian. I even remember what *I* wore!

12

A young philosopher, sitting in a garden, his life weakened by liquor and lust, heard a voice saying, "Take and read." Augustine later wrote about it happening on *that* day, at *that* time, in *that* place.

Saul of Tarsus was smitten on a particular road, on a particular day, at a particular time, on a particular errand.

John Wesley's wonderful witness of the Spirit occurred on a particular day of the week (Wednesday, May 24), at a particular time (8:45 p.m.), on a particular street (Aldersgate), in a particular city (London), with a particular people (Peter Boler and some Moravians).

And this precious promise of the Holy Spirit came in a particular and specific way as well. It was 50 days after the resurrection, ten days after the ascension, in the upper room, in Jerusalem, some time before 9 a.m. with the waiting disciples. There was a sound of wind, the sight of cloven tongues of fire, and a speaking in other languages. Important events are enhanced with detail.

So we rejoice that the result of the tarrying, the praying, and the obedience of the disciples was the promised Holy Spirit. What glorious consequences accompanied the event. Remember, these were less-than-perfect disciples of the Lord. They had been cantankerous, frightened, vacillating followers of Jesus, and now they react as men possessed — as indeed they were — possessed of the mighty power and presence of the Holy Spirit! They went everywhere preaching the Word and witnessing for the Savior. Peter stood to preach on that Day of Pentecost and under the power of the Holy Spirit such conviction fell upon the hearers that 3,000 souls gave themselves to the Savior.

We would do well to remember that conditions do not always have to be the best for God to do his mighty works. My husband John and I were scheduled to preach a revival in a certain city some time ago. The pastor who had invited us for the mission some three years before was suddenly appointed to another church, in December before our January series. The chairperson of evangelism had heart by-pass surgery two weeks previous to the meeting. Ten days before the revival, the new pastor had emergency gallbladder surgery and was too ill to take charge. Four days before the mission the church organist came down with a severe bout of the flu and the church music director died of a heart attack. Certainly the conditions were less than favorable for a successful revival, but we did the best we could, and people prayed earnestly, and God sent the best revival the church had known in years! It is the powerful, life-giving Spirit that always makes the difference!

Truly this is New Wine! Paul said, "Don't be drunk on wine — instead be filled with the Spirit." Let us pray for another Pentecost in our church and in our time! True, *we* cannot duplicate the work of God. In fact, it is difficult to duplicate anything that is successful. I read of a woman who hired two men to do some yard work. The day they came, she was having a bridge party. During the afternoon, one of her guests looked out the window to see one man raking in the yard, while the other man was performing majestic leaps and spirals in the air. "Hey! Would you look at that!" she called to her friends. One of the women said, "What a wonderful gymnast he is. I'd pay him $100 to perform for our aerobics class." The hostess opened the window and called to the fellow raking the grass to ask if he thought his friend would like the job. The man yelled to his partner to ask him, "Hey, Fred! Do you think for $100 you could step on that rake one more time?" Just so impossible is it to imitate or duplicate the events of Pentecost in our day, but we *do* know that God would like to send a fresh outpouring of his New Wine into our thirsty souls and refill us with his own dear, divine Self. It will take for us just what it took for those early disciples: waiting, prayer, unity, obedience, and consecration to God's will.

This New Wine Makes A Difference

While preaching a revival in Florida, a man told me that, as a young man, he had played with Artie Shaw's band. His

14

father had been a concert pianist, but neither of them knew the first thing about Christian music. One day the young man was invited by a friend to play his trumpet at a huge Billy Sunday evangelistic crusade. He did it, and then, at the close of the service, as he stood there watching Billy Sunday pray with those who had responded to the call, the great evangelist looked up, saw him, came over to him, and said, "Young man, have you consecrated that trumpet to God?" "I had no idea what he was talking about — consecrate. So when I shook my head, Billy Sunday took me to an old wooden folding chair, laid my trumpet on it, put his hands — one on the horn and the other on my shoulder — and prayed and gave us both to God." Then the man continued, "And you know, Barbara, it made a difference. It made a difference the way I played that trumpet and it made a difference in *me*!" The Holy Spirit does make a difference. He makes a *big* difference! Let him fill you today. Drink deeply of this Divine Wine for all occasions. There is no telling what he will do for you, with you, and through you!

Holy Wisdom
From On High!

A few years ago I was asked to preach at a large event in Atlanta. I inquired as to the theme of the occasion, and the pastor who invited me said, "I want you to preach as if it were your last sermon. If you had only one more opportunity to proclaim the Word, what message would it be? Preach that!" What a quandary! What should I preach? I first thought to preach about the omnipotence and love of God the Father. Then I reconsidered, "But I *must* preach about Jesus, his death and resurrection and the salvation he offers to the world." But, I realized as I continued to think about it, I simply could not leave out the Holy Spirit, for he is the indwelling God who quickens, instructs, and empowers the Christian. But all of this was far too much for any one sermon. Who is able to adequately handle such enormous truth in one brief half-hour? That is also the huge dilemma of preaching on Holy Trinity Sunday. We need them all: God the Father, God the Son, and God the Holy Spirit.

Our survival as Christians is impossible without all of the Godhead — this Three-in-one God of ours is absolutely essential to us. The Trinity is the doctrine that identifies us as Christian. No other religion holds to or teaches this. The Trinity gives balance to our understanding of God.

In this text in Proverbs, Wisdom, which is a Divine attribute, is expressed as a person (a woman, strangely enough). Wisdom is often used in scripture to express God's self-disclosure. Wisdom, then, is one of the many ways in which God reveals himself to us. What a desperate need there is in our time for wisdom. We have access to a plethora of knowledge. Books and information abound. No one need lack for knowledge if s/he cares to search for it. There is little excuse for ignorance. But this is not the same as wisdom.

We speak of persons who are knowledgeable, astute, brilliant, ingenious, and clever (even crafty). But knowledge does not necessarily make one wise. Did you hear about the man who learned that 80 percent of all accidents happen within two miles of home — so he moved? He had knowledge, the facts, but no wisdom for application of those facts. Some scholars are brilliant, and in their field have no peer, but still lack the wisdom of practicality. Many persons are clever, but they may not also have the wisdom to be good. They may only be "clever devils." In fact, it is doubtful if any person can have true wisdom apart from God. A good person may have wisdom and also have great knowledge, or a wise person may be short on knowledge. There is a goodness, prudence, and circumspection which alone comes from knowing God. The Psalmist said, "The fear of the Lord is the beginning of wisdom" (Psalm 111:10). Paul stated it another way, "In Christ are hidden all the treasures of wisdom and knowledge" (Colossians 2:3). He also charged young Timothy to study the scriptures "which are able to make you wise for salvation through faith in Christ Jesus" (2 Timothy 3:15).

In J. S. Bach's masterpiece, *Jesu, Joy Of Man's Desiring,* he called Jesus the "holy wisdom from on high." What does this Wisdom mean as related to the Trinity? What does it do for us today?

God The Father

God the Father is the Omniscient One: all-wise, all-knowing. Nothing escapes his eye. He was wise enough to create the universe. The Bible announces that Creation was the work of God. The story is told that Franklin D. Roosevelt and one of his close friends, Bernard Baruch, talked late into the night one evening at the White House. At last, President Roosevelt suggested that they go out into the Rose Garden and look at the stars before going to bed. They went out and looked into the sky for several minutes, peering at a nebula with thousands of stars. Then the President said, "All right, I think we feel small enough now to go in and go to sleep." The wonder of the power and wisdom of God puts things in perspective for us humans. It was not an accident, but the result of a Divine Plan; planets, stars, plants, birds, fish, and animals were all created by God.

And the climax of God's creation was humanity. How complex and mind-boggling is our physical construction. Chemically, the body is unequalled for complexity. Each one of its 30 trillion cells is a mini chemical factory that performs about 10,000 chemical functions. With its 206 bones, 639 muscles, 4 million pain sensors in the skin, 750 million air sacs in the lungs, 16 million nerve cells and 30 trillion cells in total, the human body is remarkably designed for life. And the brain! The human brain and nervous system is the most complex arrangement of matter anywhere in the universe. One scientist estimated that our brain, on the average, processes over 10,000 thoughts and concepts each day. One could spend years just dealing with the marvelous intricacies and majesty of God's creation. We are, as the Psalmist states "fearfully and wonderfully made."

For us, personally, it says that if God has the wisdom to create all we know of this world, then he also has the power and wisdom to care for us. Is there anything too hard for God? Is there any problem we have too complex? Is there any difficulty that his wisdom cannot solve? The answer is a resounding "no!" Our all-wise Creator God is also our all-sufficient heavenly Father! God, in his "holy Wisdom from on high" can make something even out of our nothingness. Don't despair! There is hope for you yet!

An unusual woman was being interviewed by a reporter. She had been a widow for years, and had reared six children of her own and 12 adopted children. In spite of her busy and useful life, she was noted for her poise and charm. The reporter asked how she had managed, amidst poverty, work, and responsibility to do it all with such a great and confident spirit. "You see," she answered, "I'm in a partnership. One day, a long time ago, I said, 'Lord, I'll do the work, and you do the worrying,' and I haven't had a worry since!" God, in his love and wisdom has promised to never leave us nor forsake us, so that we can at least have enough wisdom to trust that his wisdom is working on our behalf.

God The Son

Wisdom and truth were personified in God the Son, Jesus our Lord. Christ's death on the cross exemplified the wisdom of God in bringing about redemption for all of humanity. What other love and wisdom could ever have actualized a way for all estranged sinners to be made right with God?

Christ's life on earth manifested the wisdom of God. When his enemies tried to catch him with trick questions, his wisdom stopped them dead in their tracks. His answer was always, "a holy Wisdom from on high." They said of him, "Never a man spake like this man." Of course his words were wise, for he always spoke only truth. He said of himself, "I am the Way, the TRUTH, and the Life." How can we who follow him do less than endeavor to always speak the truth? Wisdom would surely dictate that we exercise great care in speaking only that which is honest and true. Cordell Hull, the American Secretary of State from 1933 to 1944, was reputed to be an extremely honest and cautious man, ungiven to advancing anything that was not strictly true. If there was not sufficient evidence, he was slow in forming an absolute opinion. Once, on a train trip, Hull and a companion watched while the train dragged its load of cars slowly past a large flock of sheep. Making conversation, Hull's friend said, "Those sheep have been recently sheared." Hull thoughtfully stared at the animals, then said, "It appears so. At least on the side facing us." Such cautious wisdom must have been a good trait for a secretary of state. Such wisdom would be advantageous for us as we walk in the footsteps of our Lord who is Truth exemplified.

It is perhaps his "holy Wisdom from on high" which resulted in the incarnation. Humans need human contact, and we could never understand nor know God until God was enfleshed and came among us. He walked as a man among us that we might know the loving compassion of the heart of God which felt for each of us in our need. The true story is told of a woman named Mamie who made frequent trips to the branch post office. One day she confronted a long line of people who were waiting for service from the postal clerk. Mamie only needed stamps, so a helpful observer asked her, "Why don't you just use the stamp machine? You can get all the stamps you need and you won't have to wait in line." Mamie said, "I know, but the machine can't ask me about my arthritis." That's part of the wisdom of Christ's coming to our earth to live among us. He could relate to us in all of our daily needs.

As we try to walk in Jesus' steps, we might do well to pray the ancient Irish poem set to an Irish ballad tune, which says,

> *Be Thou my Wisdom, and Thou my true Word;*
> *I ever with Thee and Thou with me, Lord;*
> *Heart of my own heart, whatever befall,*
> *Still be my Vision, O Ruler of all.*

God The Holy Spirit

And what would we ever do without the "holy Wisdom from on high," who, as the ever-present Holy Spirit, guides us into all truth? We are so shortsighted and dull without the Spirit who gives us eyes to see. An English teacher of a sophomore high school class put a small chalk dot on the blackboard. He then asked the class what it was. A few seconds passed and then someone said, "That is a chalk dot on the blackboard." The rest of the class seemed relieved that the obvious had been stated, and no one else had anything to say. "I'm surprised at you," the teacher told the class. "I did the same exercise yesterday with a group of kindergartners and they thought of 50 different things the chalk mark could be: an owl's eye, a cigar butt, the top of a telephone pole, a star, a pebble, a squashed bug, a rotten egg, a bird's eye, and so on." The older students had learned how to find a right answer, but had lost the ability to look for more than one right answer. The Holy Spirit helps us, in his wonderful Wisdom, to see more than we might have seen by ourselves. The Spirit's vision allows us wonderful options for expansion and new possibilities.

It is the Spirit's Wisdom that reveals the Word to us. It is the Wisdom of the Spirit that shows us our sin, which guides us, which instructs us, which leads us in the way everlasting. Wisdom is, in fact, one of the gifts of the Holy Spirit. Such Wisdom is beyond all human logic or knowledge or acumen or understanding. This gift of Wisdom is often accompanied by the fruits of the same Spirit which include patience and long-suffering. A pastor friend tells of a father taking his little toddler to the mall with him. The little guy was still in his "terrible twos" and was acting the part. But all the while he was yelling and crying and grabbing and screaming, you could hear his father saying to himself, "It's okay, George, you are going to be fine. Be patient, George. Cool it, George." A lady overheard his remarks and said, "You sure are patient with little George." The harried father responded, "Lady, *that's* Matthew, *I'm* George!" We might also conclude that along with the Spirit's Wisdom is given to us the fruit of self-control!

You see, there is a perception and discernment which is not inherent within us by nature. But the Spirit's perception gives a keenness and astuteness that we can never claim as our own. It is rather that wonderful, divine Wisdom from him which quickens the believer. John and I were invited to preach for a week on the campus at the Union College in Barbourville, Kentucky. While there, we were asked to make some taped messages to be aired at a later date. We were taken to the studio by a member of the faculty, and then later he took us to see a Bible camp in the mountains. Bruce Martin, the professor, had come from New York City, and while there, had been an artist on the piano. He had magic fingers, and his touch and skill were breathtaking. After his conversion to Christ, he had come to teach at Union College. While looking over the camp we came to a room where there was an old piano. The room was dusty, messy, junky, and cold, but it was the old piano in the corner that caught Bruce's attention. Half the keys had ivories missing, the front panel was gone, exposing the inner workings of the instrument, and it looked literally like it needed to be on a trash heap somewhere. He sat down at the piano and began to play the battered thing and immediately the whole place came alive. The surroundings were literally transformed! Such beautiful music came out of that piano that we felt as if we were standing in the middle of a miracle. God's presence radiated within that dark room, and tears filled our eyes as we listened to the music from the hands of an artist. It was his touch that made all the difference! So, too, is the touch of the Spirit upon our lives. From somewhere beyond ourselves he pours music from our broken lives and lets a fallen world see what God can do with nothing when it is given to him and to his control.

Such then, is the Wisdom of Proverbs — a "holy Wisdom from on high." May God impart its wondrous beauty to each of our lives that our own personal needs may be met and that we may be empowered to serve the world that Christ died to save.

Priest
Without Peer

We are about to behold a priest without peer. Just to say the word priest or preacher brings to mind all kinds of stories where the clergy became the laughing stock of the joke. Such as: A bus driver and a priest died at the same time. Although the bus driver was sent directly to heaven, the priest's case was apparently harder to decide. "I don't mind that you sent a bus driver to heaven," the priest complained, "but, after all, I was a priest, so why should I be kept waiting?" He was answered by a voice from on high, "Father, when you were preaching, everyone was falling asleep, but when the bus driver was driving, everyone was praying."

One of my best friends, when I was a pastor in Missouri, was the Roman Catholic priest who ministered in the same town as I. He was Irish, had a sense of humor that was both gentle and hilarious, and was one of the most deeply committed to Christ ministers that I have ever known. But not all priests are of such godly character. The news has recently been filled with the scandal of priests who sexually abuse children and in other ways violate the vocation that is theirs. The sad truth is that "bad apples" are in every area of society's leadership; it just appears much worse when it is a minister of the Gospel of the Lord Jesus Christ who is guilty. People expect more (and have a right to), of those who have been

25

ordained and set apart for the administration of Word and sacraments, and it is tragic when such are found to betray that high and holy calling.

Today's text deals with a superior priest. He is named Melchizedek, King of Salem. Three times he is mentioned in the Bible: in this text, in Psalm 110:4, and in three chapters in Hebrews. As difficult and enigmatic as this passage in Genesis is, it is still rich in typology when we untangle its knotty meaning. Abraham's encounter with Melchizedek can be seen as a type of our Lord Jesus Christ.

The verse in the 110th Psalm, "You are a priest forever in the order of Melchizedek," was given a Christological reading early in the Christian church. In fact, this passage is the middle ground which establishes a link between our text and the New Testament mention of him. Melchizedek, then, is the prototype of the only real high priest we Christians have: Jesus our Lord.

What Melchizedek did for Abraham, Jesus, our High Priest, does for us. However, Christ does far, far more.

Refreshment With Bread And Wine

Melchizedek refreshed Abraham with bread and wine. Abraham had just experienced a great victory over the five kings of Sodom, and now, after the conflict, this man of faith was refreshed by the appearance of Melchizedek.

Melchizedek brought out bread and wine to Abraham and blessed him. Jesus, our High Priest, our heavenly Melchizedek, brings out bread and wine, but because Christ is so far superior to Melchizedek, he offers us his own body and blood. Christ first gave the precious body and blood as he offered himself on Calvary's tree for our sins, and that redemption, so dearly purchased, redeems us as we bow in repentance and faith at his cross. As our Mediator and Intercessor, he continues to pray and intercede for us at the Father's right hand in heaven. With poignant understanding of this great sacrifice,

Charles Wesley wrote:

Five bleeding wounds he bears, received on Calvary;
They pour effectual prayers, They strongly plead for me.
"Forgive him, O, forgive!" they cry, "Nor let that ran-
somed sinner die."

And still our High Priest continues to refresh us at his table as we partake of the bread and wine of holy communion.
There, again, we find forgiveness for our sins. No other priest,
no other mediator, offers so much to those who are so un-
worthy. Alexander Whyte, that prince of preachers in St.
George's Church, Edinburgh, in the early years of this century, once told of attending a service of holy communion conducted by John Duncan, the well-known Scottish divine of an
earlier day. Noticing a woman shake her head when the elder
passed the cup to her while tears ran down her cheeks, Dr.
Duncan stepped down from behind the altar table and taking
the cup from the elder, he passed it to the woman and said,
"Take it, woman, for it is for sinners." What good news for
all of us that is: Christ still receiveth sinners and eateth with
them, offering his own self to renew our souls. Coca Cola may
be the "pause that refreshes," but this refreshment from our
heavenly High Priest restores and energizes us for the journey of life as no other bread and wine can do!

Melchizedek Blessed Abraham

Then, having given him bread and wine, Melchizedek
blessed Abraham in the name of the most High, Creator of
heaven and earth. And what a rich blessing it was! His words
spoken that day became a standard liturgical formula in Israel. In fact, it became a doxology of praise! Interesting, isn't
it, that all of the creation of the Creator seems to want to sing
his praise! Warbling birds in early dawn seem to proclaim their
joy in being a part of God's handiwork. According to research

27

conducted by the National Geographic Society, the 40-ton creation of God, the humpback whale, has a fascinating singing ability. Recordings have been made of the whale singing in various pitches in solos, duets, trios, and choruses of dozens of interweaving voices, lasting from 6 to 30 minutes. What an experience it is to hear, over one's stereo system, songs from the deep of the ocean sung by these whales. The passage comes to mind, "Praise him down here on earth you creatures of the ocean depths" (Psalm 148:7).

Melchizedek's blessing was actually a doxology that reminds us of our "Praise God From Whom All Blessings Flow" hymn. In fact, there are five passages in the Psalms which use this same doxology spoken by Melchizedek. Though these words name God as Creator, they not so much emphasize a concern over how the world came to be, but rather what God, who did create, wants to do for us. It is a "given" that God made everything, but this blessing reminds us that the God who did this is a reality *now*, and that he makes a difference in our present!

The Blessing Brings Help

As Melchizedek gave the blessing, and then the psalmist echoed it again and again, we begin to see how involved God wants to be with us. Most of us have little trouble believing how involved God wants to be with us. Most of us have little trouble believing that the Omnipotent God created our marvelous universe. Our problem arises out of our doubt that such a One could be interested in our finite selves and our individual situations.

Dr. Robert Stackel tells of an old man who lived on the street and who one day became very ill and was rushed to the hospital. The doctors realized he could not live very long. They tried to find the old man's name, but all the old man would say was, "Son! Son!" In looking through his clothing for identification, they could only find a news clipping about a marine

who was stationed in Korea. The Red Cross located this marine and flew him back to the United States and to the hospital. As the young man walked into the hospital room, the old man smiled broadly and exclaimed, "Son!" For several hours the young man sat by the bed and held the old man's hand until he died peacefully. After his death the nurse said to the marine, "We need to know your father's full name." The marine replied, "He wasn't my father. I never saw the man before in my life." Amazed, the nurse asked, "Then why did you stay?" The boy answered, "Because he needed me." When the psalmist prayed Melchizedek's blessing (Psalm 121:2), he found, as do we, real comfort and assurance in a present God. "My *help* comes from the Lord, Maker of heaven and earth." Henry F. Lyte knew God was a present help when he wrote:

> *When other helpers fail, and comforts flee,*
> *Help of the helpless, O abide with me.*

Some time ago I attended the large wedding of a nephew. My sister-in-law, Mary Louise, had recommended her hairdresser as someone who would shampoo and set my hair for me. Stephen, her hairdresser, who was Greek Orthodox, was nervous and excited over the big event, and was taking his responsibilities very seriously. He had never done my hair before, of course, and was so afraid he would not do it right. I assured him that it would be fine, but he still couldn't get it done to his own satisfaction. He worked and worked, and became more and more agitated. Finally, he excused himself and disappeared for a couple of minutes, then returned and went back to work. Soon I heard him whisper to himself, "Thank the Lord, I think I'm getting it." I asked him, not really expecting an affirmative answer, "What did you do, Stephen — go pray?" "Oh, yes," he readily agreed. "See that picture of the Lord over there. I went over and kissed Jesus and asked for his help!" The truth is, God is always on-call to help us when we need his Divine aid.

In the days of the romantic sailing vessels, the three signal flags B.N.C. meant, "I will not abandon you." This was the most important promise a ship could make as it drew up alongside of its distressed sister ship which it had come to help. It meant life, help, courage, and the promise that a friend was near. In much the same way, God has made the cross of Christ his signal flag to distressed humanity. He will not abandon us, nor leave us, nor forsake us .... "Our help comes from the Lord."

Who of us is ever so independent that we do not need the aid of another? But sometimes the "other" is unwilling to help us, or too weak, or too busy. That is never the case with our all-sufficient High Priest. It is said of him again and again in the scriptures, "He is able! He is able! He is able! Able to help, able to deliver, able to save, able to heal, able to forgive — He is able!"

The Doxology Is A Blessing

Melchizedek's doxology is spoken by the psalmist as a blessing from God: "May the Lord of heaven and earth bless you from Zion" (Psalm 134:3). More than any other verses in Genesis do these words of Melchizedek invite us to take our faith out of worrying about "creation origins," and believe that God would like to *bless us*! He is our Source, not only for life, but also for buoyancy, and even joy in the trials of our way.

Because God is God, he can both curse and he can bless. Woe to those whom God curses, whether it be an individual or nation! It is devastating when the curse and the judgment of God falls upon the disobedient, upon the blasphemer, and upon the unrepentant. God's eyes are ever upon us: upon those who do evil and those who do good. He never sleeps; nothing escapes him. He is not hoodwinked by our easy rationalizations for our sins. He misses nothing. He knows the thoughts of our hearts. He interprets all we do in the light of his commands. We almost find ourselves agreeing with Dennis the Menace in a cartoon which shows him leaving the church with his parents saying, "If God is always watching me, he must catch me being good *once* in a while!'' How happy we are when God can bless our lives as we try to follow him in obedience and integrity.

It is always grace, mercy, love, and unspeakable joy when God blesses. His loving benediction is all we ever need or desire. A young minister, having preached his sermon, raised his hand and began the benediction, ''Go in hope, and offer hope to all of God's people. Go in peace, and make peace to all of God's people. Go in love, and make love to all of ... Oh, well, you know what I mean. Amen.'' But the true benediction and blessing of God upon us is glorious indeed. How wonderful it is, as we leave the house of worship on Sunday, to hear the pastor say this familiar blessing for us, on God's behalf: ''The Lord bless you and keep you, the Lord make his face to shine upon you and be gracious to you, the Lord look upon you with favor, and grant you peace.''

No doubt about it: Jesus, our great Melchizedek, our High Priest and Mediator, is superior to all others! He is our Priest without peer! Christ is greater, for his credentials are based upon his death and glorious resurrection. Melchizedek is no more, Christ is forever! Christ stands above all other priests because of the power of his indestructible life (Hebrews 7:25).

None can ever compare to this matchless, incomparable, and unique Priest of ours. Of whom else could it ever be said, ''He is able to save *completely* those who come to God through him, because he always lives to intercede for them'' (Hebrews 7:25)? So, Christians, why be anxious? Why be full of worry and care? Your High Priest comes to meet you with wounded hands, to refresh and help and bless!

The "No-Contest" Contest

When my husband and I play tennis it is a "no-contest" contest. He is a far better player than I. In fact, we have a deal that anytime I can beat him a whole set, he will take me out for a lobster dinner. He is perfectly safe from having to pay. This contest has been running for as long as we've been married, and in 21 years I've had lobster once! The match is a "no-contest" contest. He *always* wins!

In this text we have another kind of competition. The contest takes place on Mount Carmel. There is a sharp rivalry between Elijah and the pagan prophets, between God and Baal, between true and false gods. But the outcome will show it to be another "no-contest" contest.

God Wants To Be Your Only God

Elijah, the prophet of God, has just announced to King Ahab and the people of Israel that they must choose between worshipping the pagan gods and the Lord God of Israel. They can no longer divide their loyalties between God and his idols. The prophet's question, "How long will you go limping between two different opinions?" points out how truly disabled they are. Then Elijah commands, "If the Lord is God, follow Him; but if Baal, then follow him."

He then proposes a test to see which God they will worship. The choice they make must be clean-cut. They do *not* have the option to keep straddling the fence, serving God one day and Baal the next. The selections are not *both*, only one of two: God or Baal.

These have always been the only two alternatives we've been given — and to fail to choose God is *always* to choose Baal — or some other false god. God wants us to learn the lesson of how worthless all other gods are. The God of the Bible insists on exclusive loyalty. In fact, the first of the ten commandments is an emphatic and absolute rule: "Thou shalt have *no other* gods before me!"

Joshua had made the same challenge. After the death of Moses he called for a renewal of the covenant and said, "Now if you are unwilling to serve the Lord, choose this day whom ye will serve ... but as for me and my household, we will serve the Lord." Until you are sure about God, you are unsure about nearly everything else. No one is as flighty and inconsistent and irresolute as that person who cannot or has not decided who is to be his/her God. James reminds us that "to be double-minded is to be unstable in everything."

Today we live in a time when every "ism," sect, and religion which comes down the pike offers a "new God" to us. Some people feel they must sample them all. So we have the Eastern religions, new age, humanism, secularism, and a plethora of strange sects, all promoting their own private brand of God. A lady told me recently, "I've finally worked out a theology about God all on my own. It leaves me lots of options and plenty of leeway, it makes no demands and carries no judgment, and best of all, it feels good. What do you think of that?" The truth is that she is not a lot different from what everyone else does who opts for a god other than the God shown to us in the Bible. And that God is revealed clearly to us in the person of his only Son. Luther was right on target when he said, "I know of no other God except the God whom I see in my Lord Jesus Christ." We are only kidding ourselves if we think we can opt for a convenient "God of the hour." A

New Yorker cartoon showed one of those shaggy, slightly sinister drawings revealing a mixed bunch of our American contemporaries who had recently arrived in hell. They were being addressed by an affable devil, complete with pitchfork, horns, and tail. "You'll find there's no right or wrong here," he says, "just do whatever works for you." We would all do well to heed the words of Saint Augustine who said, "Before God can deliver us from ourselves we must first undeceive ourselves."

God's word warns that all such choices, other than the true God, are apostasy. Apostasy is deserting the Lord God, becoming faithless to him, and abandoning the faith of our fathers. That is exactly what the nation of Israel had done, and now God is calling them back to making a definite choice. God clearly punishes apostasy. He will be God of all or God not at all. Actually, the Israelites had settled for syncretism. They sought to simply combine and reconcile the different beliefs: a little of the Hebrew God and a little of the pagan gods, mix them according to personal taste, and worship the result. But Elijah said, "No way!" God is an exclusive God, he knows that all other gods are worthless. The point is that God is God, period! The psalmist said, "My heart is *fixed*, O God, on Thee" (Psalm 108:1).

Have you ever wondered what would happen if God would be your God — your *only* God? Not money, not your children, not your spouse, not sex, not power, not your job, not sports, not self — but God and God alone? Wow! What a difference it would make in your entire life, for God rewards fidelity and God fights all the battles for those who truly make him Lord of all.

Oswald Chambers wrote, "Never try to explain God till you have obeyed him. The only bit of God we understand is the bit we have obeyed." There is a wondrous confidence and reassurance in choosing, knowing, and obeying the Lord God of the scriptures. We need then recognize only one voice, obey only one Master, and follow only one standard. Let the clamor of all other gods sound about us, our trust is in the Lord who changes not and who ever abideth faithful. God wants to be your only God, but once you have chosen him, you see how powerless, puny, and helpless all other gods can be. It is truly a "no-contest" contest.

God Wants To Answer Your Prayers

Elijah then proposes a test to see which god they will worship.Two altars will be built, two sacrifices will be made, and the God who consumes the sacrifices with fire will be declared the winner of the contest.

The prophets of Baal are given every advantage in the contest. They get to go first. Thus Elijah can never be accused of rigging the results in his favor.

The contest begins in the early morning with 450 prophets of Baal. It was easy enough to prepare the sacrifice and lay it on the altar, but getting an answer from Baal is something else! Then begin the long hours of vain crying — of course it is vain for heathenism has no true prayer. They howled, they cried, they raved, they pled, they begged, they cut themselves with swords and lances until they bled, but silence was their only answer.

The day wore on, their voices grew hoarse; and Elijah taunted them as he suggested that their god must be tired, or resting, or asleep, or on a journey.

As the evening shadows begin to lengthen, the scriptures point out with poignant and vivid simplicity how futile is their cause, for it says of their wild, frantic, all-day endeavors, "There was no voice, no answer, no response."

Then the wild commotion turns to holy calm. The sun is sinking behind the peak of Mount Carmel, and Elijah, with his own hands, repairs the ruined altar of Jehovah. He rebuilds it with 12 stones, representing the 12 tribes of Israel. He then places the sacrifice upon the altar. Next he calls for four barrels of water to be poured on the sacrifice to soak it, and then four more barrels, and then four more: 12 in all. The water

36

drenches the sacrifice, runs down the altar, and fills the trench all about it. A totally saturated sacrifice.

Then Elijah prays: a simple, brief prayer of only about 60 words. Notice — no screaming, no wailing, no self-inflicted wounds — just a calm confidence as he addresses his prayer with adoration of the name of Jehovah and requests the fire to fall. Note, too, that this prophet had no exalted opinion of himself, for he reminded God that he was only doing what God had told him to do. He then requests that in God's answer the people would once again know God and fasten their hearts on him.

Elijah's prayer did what the all-day crying of the pagans could never do. God answered! God sent fire! The fire consumed the sacrifice, and the altar, and the stones, and the dust, and even the water in the trench!

Elijah's God still lives today and answers prayer with power. God craves to answer our prayers and meet our needs. A study of Elijah's prayer and then using it as an example for ourselves would be helpful in getting results from heaven too.

Bear in mind that Elijah did exactly what God wanted him to do. He said in his prayer, "I did all these things at your command." How often do we pray powerless prayers and without faith for we know we have been disobedient to God's command? Guilt makes for feeble faith. There is nothing that so quickly feeds faith and opens heaven's doors as a true repentance when we have sinned. Then follows a quiet assurance that God hears us when we lift our needs to him. What Elijah asked was virtually impossible as far as humanity was concerned, but Elijah knew that nothing was too big for God, nor too impossible. Many persons are afraid to pray because they are afraid they will ask God to do something he cannot do. But if God is God, then be realistic. Ask the impossible!

A few months ago my husband John took a man to see the doctor. His wife had requested it because she was confined to a wheelchair, and therefore was unable to do it for him. The man was very weak and could hardly make the trip, but did manage to see the doctor who sent him home with other medication. Two days later John got the word that the man had died, so he went to visit the wife and offer sympathy. After visiting a while, John asked her, "Would you like me to have prayer with you and for you?" He did not know they were of the Jewish faith, until her response. She said, "Oh, yes! I would be so glad if you would pray. I need it so much." Then she added, "The rabbi came to visit my husband a few hours before he died and my husband asked the rabbi if he would offer a prayer for him. The rabbi hesitated a long while, pondered, and then said, 'Well, I guess I could pray if you think it would do any good.' " Let it forever be known as an absolute truth that it *does* do good to pray! God *does* hear prayer. God *does* answer prayer. It has been my experience that God does not always give us exactly what we request, but he *does* always answer, usually in one of four ways. He may say, "Yes," "No," "Wait," or "I'm going to surprise you with something better." But always he gives us what is for our highest and best good. Count on it!

Notice the simplicity of Elijah's prayer. Clear, to the point, and only about 60 words. We so often complicate things. A wife reported to her husband that she was having trouble with her car; it had water in the carburetor. Her husband laughed and said, "That's ridiculous. It doesn't have water in the carburetor. Besides, you don't even know what a carburetor is. Where is the car?" She replied, "It's in the swimming pool!"

We, too, muddle things with intricate complications when we pray, but it is not necessary. Little children often point us the way to simplicity in prayer. They have a way of getting right to the heart of things without undue confusion. One little boy, named Peter, prayed, "Dear God, that fairy you sent left five cents for my tooth and a quarter for my brother. You still owe me 20 cents." A little girl thought to make it clear how God could improve things, so she prayed, "Dear God, the people in the next apartment fight real loud all the time. You should only let very good friends get married. Nan."

And Elijah's prayer was selfless. He had the best of motives. He said, "Answer me, so these people will know that you, O Lord, are God." He wanted God to be glorified, his name to be honored. There was nothing of self nor selfishness in his prayer. God answered, and fire fell from heaven!

God is God, and he longs for his people to call upon him. So often we have made God smaller than he is. We've said, "Now that we have penicillin we can do without prayer. Let's have Medicare and Medicaid and we can live without mercy. Give us sulfa and forget salvation. Give us finance and we can do without faith. If we have gold we don't need God."

But we *do* need God. We *cannot* and *must* not try to live without prayer. Dr. Randy Byrd, a San Francisco cardiologist, has done a double-blind, randomized, study of prayer relating to 393 coronary care unit patients in San Francisco General Hospital. (Double-blind means that neither patients nor doctors knew who was being prayed for. All were in the same comparable age group and same comparable condition. They were impartially chosen by a computer.) Dr. Byrd arranged for prayer groups to pray for 192 of the patients, but not for 201 others. The patients who were subjects of prayer suffered fewer complications. Only three required antibiotics, 16 of the "unprayed for" needed the drug. Only six of the prayed for suffered pulmonary edema, while 18 of the nonprayed for did. There was 20 percent faster recovery, for those prayed for. One of the prayed for died, 16 of the unremembered died. When we are sick, or at any other time in our lives, it remains true that the quickest way to get back on your feet is to get down on your knees.

It's A "No-Contest" Contest

There can be no doubt about it. It's a "no-contest" contest: you always get along better when you pray! And, the fact is, the "no-contest" contest on Mount Carmel was never a battle between two competing gods. Instead, it was a contest between God and an empty delusion.

The results were in long before the competition began. You need to know that when you fight God you lose *every* time, and when you trust and obey, you are the victor *every* time!

Proper 5
Pentecost 3
Ordinary Time 10
1 Kings 17:8-16 (17-24)

Hard
Questions!

Children sometimes ask cute questions, but often they are also incisive. In *Children's Letters to God*, a child inquires, "Dear God, Where does everybody come from? I hope you explain it better than my father. Ward." Another child queries, "Dear God, Did you mean for a giraffe to look like that or was it an accident? Norma." Then, there are those persons who, in the presence of larger questions, can think only of the obvious and mundane. Yellowstone Park Rangers report that, at the place where Old Faithful geyser, every hour or so, lifts its heavenly plume of water to the sky, the most frequently asked question is "Where is the bathroom?"

There are some really hard questions which deal with our faith and our spiritual lives. This narrative of Elijah and the Widow of Zarephath deals with some of them.

Whom Do You Trust?

A popular television show of a couple of decades ago asked this question, "Whom Do You Trust?" If God were to ask us, individually, whom we trust, what would our honest answer be?

41

Elijah appears in the Old Testament very abruptly. One minute you never heard of him and the next he's changing the scene about him in his brash, confident, no-nonsense, take-charge manner. Elijah's name means "Yahweh is my God." This man, whose very name is a glad confession of faith, will bring hope to God's people who have been often oppressed. In this story their troubles come from King Ahab. Elijah is going to surprise the discouraged with encouragement, and the nation is going to realize once more that God's power is available to help them and that his heart is more than willing to feel their needs.

Now Elijah, this man under orders, this man under a command from the word of God, is sent — not to the king, nor one of the priests, not to anybody of importance — but to a nobody. He is dispatched to a person of insignificance in that society, the Widow of Zarephath. Oddly enough, he is commissioned to go to her, not to help her, but to ask for help himself. He is sent, not to feed, but to be fed! Imagine! A Gentile woman will feed a Hebrew prophet! How markedly different are the ways of God from ours.

When Elijah arrives in Zarephath he finds the woman at the town gate, gathering wood. He requests her to bring him a drink of water, and then, almost as an afterthought, asks her to bring him some bread also. This foreigner tells Elijah she hasn't any bread. In fact, due to the lack of rain in the land, the earth has not produced for many months and she has only enough olive oil in a jar and meal in a barrel to bake a small cake for herself and her son. She further explains that at that very moment she was gathering sticks to build a fire upon which to bake the last meal they will have before they starve to death.

Now note the audacity of this man of God. He commands her, "Don't worry! Make the cake and bring it to me first and I promise you that you'll always have oil in your cruse and meal in your barrel until God sends rain again upon the land."

It was a real test of faith in the word of the Lord, through Elijah, that asked for her to give the prophet the cake first, even before feeding her son. I wonder if a part of the lesson here is to realize that God doesn't desire our leftovers. He deserves the first and the best, simply because he is God. If you had been this poor woman would you have believed this man whose name means "Yahweh is my God"? Would you have trusted God to be telling the truth through Elijah? Remember, this is a life and death situation. It's no time for small talk or games. Would you have risked your own life and the life of your son in this circumstance? Would you have felt the stakes were too high to gamble on such an important decision? Is a simple, plain word from God enough in such a serious affair? Would you have taken this leap of faith? This is a hard question and pushes each of us back to the ultimate, "Whom *do* you trust?"

There is a kind of wild and wonderful optimism and faith in the person who believes God can help in any situation, no matter how extreme. A client asked an attorney in Louisiana to research the title to a piece of property he was considering buying, and told the lawyer he needed it to be a very complete report before the finance corporation would grant a loan. The attorney came back with this description of the land: "Louisiana was purchased by the United States from France in 1803. France got the title by right of conquest from Spain. Spain came into possession by right of discovery in 1492 by a sailor named Christopher Columbus, who had been granted the privilege of seeking a new route to India by Queen Isabella. The queen had taken the precaution of securing the blessing of the Pope of Rome upon the voyage before she sold her jewels to help Columbus. The Pope, as you know, is the emissary of Jesus Christ, who is the Son of God, and God, it is commonly accepted, made the world, including the property in question in Louisiana!" That's about how far back you can push a Christian in response to this question — basic to our trust is the knowledge that God created the world and all that is in it. Will we trust him or a lesser deity? Would you trust modern technology or God, when the chips are down? Do you trust nuclear armaments and put your final trust in Star Wars games for life or death? Would you trust your employer, the government, or the power of high finance? Do you trust your spouse implicitly, or could s/he perhaps fail you? How about your best friend? Maybe you trust in yourself? Or is God, after all, the One you trust? Our coins read, "In God we trust." Do we, or is that just a nice slogan for hard cash? *Can* God be absolutely trusted? If so, do you?

Will You Obey?

The minister came smiling into the house one evening when I, as guest evangelist, was visiting there. I said, "What's so funny?" He said, "I just returned from calling on Aunt Mattie in our church. She's 103 years old today. I asked her how she had managed to live so long, and she just said, 'That's easy, Preacher. I just trust and obey, drink ice water and crochet.' " I'm not sure about the ice water and the crocheting, but there is no doubt that she had found the secret for joyful, Christian living. She had learned obedience. The mother of Jesus realized the importance of obeying. She told the servants at the home in Cana where the wine had run out at the wedding feast, "Whatever he says to you, *do it!*" What simple, difficult advice that was. Jesus himself came to the place of absolute obedience to the Father, when in Gethsemane he prayed, "Not my will, but thine be done."

Let us suppose that you've decided that above and beyond all other persons and things, that God is completely trustworthy. The next hard question that logically follows is, "Will you obey him?" Perfect trust always involves perfect obedience. Obedience is difficult for us because we want our own way much of the time. An overweight business executive decided he had to lose some excess pounds. He went on a strict diet, and took it very seriously. He even changed his route as he drove to work, in order to avoid the temptation to stop at his favorite bakery. One morning, the man arrived at work carrying a gigantic Danish pastry. Everyone scolded him, but he just smiled blissfully and explained, "This is a very special pastry. I accidentally drove by the bakery this morning, and there in the window was a display of all these luscious goodies. I felt this was no accident, so I prayed, 'Lord, if you want me to have one of these wonderful pastries, let me find a parking space directly in front of the bakery.' And sure enough," he smugly continued, "the eighth time around the block, there it was!"

All of us are experts at claiming to trust God, but we cop out when it comes to obedience. We want *what* we want, *when* we want it! So the hard question after "Whom do you trust?" is, "Will you obey God?" Will you do as he asks? It might have seemed to the Widow of Zarephath that God was asking far too much! He didn't say, "If you have enough left over, then give me some," but "Make me a cake *first!*" It almost seems as if God was going a bit too far, doesn't it?

Obedience is always a matter of faith, born of total trust. Archibald Rutledge told the story of meeting a black turpentine worker whose faithful dog had just died a few moments earlier in a great forest fire because he would not desert his master's dinner pail, which he had been told to watch. With tears streaming down his face, the old man said, "I always had to be careful what I told him to do, because I knowed he'd do it." Do we offer God full obedience, or do we obey only when it's handy, convenient, to our liking, and not too costly? Is God asking too much to expect me to tithe? Some would reply, "I have trouble enough making ends meet now," or "I'm on a fixed income," or, "My bills are already insurmountable. Surely God knows I can't afford to tithe." But we must not forget that Christians are people who are radically surrendered and dedicated to a Jesus who gave his all and expects anyone who follows him to give their all too. Only the commitment of entire obedience gives us identity as a disciple of his. That means in more matters than just money, too. Obedience is to take to heart, with all earnestness, the commands of Christ, "Seek ye first the kingdom of God," "If any would come after me, let him deny himself, take up his

45

cross, and follow me," and all such radical charges of our Lord. It means surrendering *my* way to *his* way.

Some years ago there was a man at the head of Duke University by the name of President Few. It is said that one Sunday he was seen walking across the campus with his umbrella raised to protect himself from the pouring rain. Some friends saw him, stopped their car, and offered him a ride. He got in, and as they drove toward the church, one of the persons in the car said, "Why did you decide to go to church in the rain this morning?" Few replied, "I didn't decide this morning. I decided 65 years ago, and I haven't had to ask myself that question since." Such holy habits become ours, too, when our minds are already made up to do his will, no matter the outer circumstances.

Scary, isn't it? What if we obey and things don't work out? What if we go out on a limb, only to find it cut off behind us? What if we leap in holy, obedient faith into the uncertain darkness to find that there's no one to catch us? What if? What if? What if? The unnamed Widow of Zarephath must have felt the same way: nervous, trembling, wanting to trust, and yet afraid. The words of Elijah came to her, "Do not fear, don't worry." His powerful pledge of assurance that God cared, that things would be better, led her to the trust of full obedience, so she made the cake for the prophet, and fed him first. And her situation *immediately* changed! Her endless cycle of poverty and need and living on the brink of starvation was broken by the intervention of God. Wonder of wonders, there was a measureless and unfailing supply of oil and meal. No matter how many cakes she baked, there was always enough and more!

Now note the progression of these hard questions. "Whom do you trust?" If it is indeed God, then it follows that we must answer the subsequent query, "Will you obey God?" If the answer to this is affirmative, then it naturally follows that we must ask,

Does It Pay?

Does it always pay to obey God? The woman has plenty of food, the hunger needs have been met, but now real disaster strikes. She must have thought her whole world was falling apart. Her dearest possession — her son — sickens and dies. That raises a lot of troubling suspicions in her mind. She as much as says to Elijah, "I fed you and gave you a place to stay, but while it's true I received help for a while, the thing I feared in the first place has now happened to me. God has let me down after all. I realize my boy did not starve to death, but sickness has killed him. In any case, he's dead! Why? Is it because of my sins?" (Guilt always leads us to suspect that our sins have led us into God's disfavor and judgment.)

It is a fact that life sometimes does seem grossly unfair and unjust. It breaks out in unexpected ways that offend and hurt. Life is often inconvenient, uncomfortable, undependable, and often beyond our control. It is in just such a difficult time that God's holy word of promise works best!

The boy is brought back from death and restored to his mother when the man of God prays for him. The widow's reaction is to conclude that God's word *is* truth. Christians still find it to be a verity; God's promises *never* fail. Because Christ *is* truth, because he cannot lie, then his Word is consistently dependable. You can stake your life on it!

Yet, like the Widow of Zarephath, our loved ones sometimes sicken and die but they are not resurrected (yet!), but in the face of our "daily deaths" of grief, fear, guilt, hatred, and loss comes the God who breaks in upon us as the Divine Life-Bringer in the midst of our dying. Does it pay then to trust God? Of course it does! There is no investment in the universe which pays such remarkable dividends as obedient trust in our living Lord. I have a minister friend who has had some extraordinarily traumatic and impossibly difficult times in his life. And yet, with beautiful simplicity and faith and obedience he says, "If God never answers another prayer for me, I'll serve and love and trust him anyway!" He has long since learned that it pays to count on God. No wonder Job was able to say, at last, "Though God slay me, yet will I trust him!" God's only Son, our Lord Jesus Christ, would come many years later, to do the will of the Father. But when doing that divine will he wound up dying on a cruel cross. In obedient trust and absolute submission he was able to say, "Father, into thy hands I commend my Spirit," and died. Did it pay? Was that trust in his Father too costly? Was his obedience lost to an indifferent Deity? Was his life of confidence doomed to failure? Was death on a tree a dead-end street? Never, never, never! Three days later God raised his trusting, obedient Son to glorious life! Even now he is seated at his Father's right hand, crowned with glory, honor, power, and exaltation. Remember, this life is not all there is.

It boils down to this: you will trust God only as much as you love him. You will love God, not because you have studied him, but because you have touched him and he has touched you. This does not mean an automatic end to all trouble in the future. Trust does not guarantee you will never again experience desolation, disappointment, or pain — but it *does* mean you never go through it alone!

These are hard questions we've considered, but the solutions are not too hard for God. God's grand reassurance to us is, "I will never leave thee nor forsake thee." What a glorious promise to our trusting obedience to a loving God.

Proper 6
Pentecost 4
Ordinary Time 11
1 Kings 21:1-10 (11-14) 15-21a

Grapes Of
Wrath Or Grace?

A musician in a camp meeting where I preached wrote a country-gospel song titled, "Sin Will Take You Farther Than You Want To Go and Keep You Longer Than You Want To Stay." Nineteen words is a tad long for a song title, but it does state a succinct and compelling truth: sin will get you in serious trouble.

In this lesson, Ahab is king and is married to the wicked, Baal-worshipping Jezebel, and covets the vineyard belonging to a worshipper of God named Naboth. Ahab had plenty of property of his own, but he wants *this* particular piece of land: probably to use for a kitchen garden, maybe for growing herbs. He offered to buy it, but Naboth refused to sell. Naboth loved this bit of land which his fathers had cultivated for more years than Ahab reigned in days. He was also obeying the law of God. According to covenant law, all land belonged to God, who graciously allowed the people of Israel to use it. The land was the people's inheritance from God, and any property was to remain in the family to which it had been given. Naboth was not afraid nor ashamed to show himself a worshipper of Yahweh — so he refused to sell his vineyard. And therein is the problem: Naboth had the land; Ahab wanted it. Ahab offered to buy; Naboth refused to sell.

49

When he didn't get his own way, Ahab went home to pout and sulk. He went to bed, turned his face to the wall, and refused to eat. How utterly weak and childish was King Ahab!

Jezebel, hearing about it, taunted Ahab a bit, and then the strong-willed, wicked woman proposed to "give" it to him herself, even though it was never hers to give. Her ploy was to frame Naboth and then to have him unjustly executed as an enemy of the state. When such a one was executed, the property inevitably fell, not to the heirs, but to the crown. So the deed was done, and as soon as Naboth was stoned to death Jezebel told her husband to go and take possession of the vineyard.

Immediately — his pouting and sulking forgotten, and like a child who finally gets its own way — Ahab went to inspect his new, ill-gotten possession. Scarcely had he arrived on the scene when Elijah, the prophet of God, appeared. The king had not seen him since the contest on Mount Carmel. Ahab's first words were, "Have you found me, O my enemy?" Elijah's answer was right to the point, "I have found you." Then Elijah continued with solemn accusation and dire warning that his sin would cost him dearly.

This chapter is a no-nonsense text and we will be wise if we learn the obvious lessons from this account.

Sin's Pleasures Are Short-Lived

Ahab really wanted that vineyard. But once he had gained it wrongfully, it turned to ashes in his hands as soon as he had it. The unattainable, once attained by wrong means was, after all, not worth the final price he had to pay.

Sin's pleasures don't last long and the cost is unbelievably high. The Bible solemnly warns that "the wages of sin is death."

When we are tempted to sin, that sin is loved, enticing, alluring, attractive, and oh, so desirable! But when sin is done it is loathed, despised, and deeply regretted.

Think of those persons who are enticed into using drugs. They are promised a "high," they will be part of the "in crowd," and all their worries will take wings. But once begun, the "high" soon results in an all-time "low," the monetary freedom becomes a permanent bondage, and the damage to body and brain is an intolerable price to pay.

Or consider the telling of a lie. It seems so simple, so much more convenient, and often easier than the truth. But once told, the habit becomes a never-ending chain of falsehoods, each larger than the last, and finally there is the terrible knowledge that no one believes you even when you do tell the truth.

Or what of the one who for one short moment of sexual gratification promiscuously indulges in illicit sex and then pays the price of contracting the disease of herpes, gonorrhea, or worst of all, AIDS?

How about the spouse who forsakes the marriage vows and commits adultery. Having thus sinned against the faithful husband or wife, against one's own body, and the partner in sin, the realization dawns that the cost is exorbitant. Perhaps the marriage falls apart, or trust is never fully regained, or the children suffer from being a part of a broken family. All of this for the short pleasures of sin!

A few years ago, the best-known pickpocket in Cleveland, Ohio, a man by the name of Louis Finkelstein, died. He was known by police officers all across the country as "Louis the Dip." For 50 years he had pursued his career of filching items from other people's pockets. The police said he must have stolen hundreds of thousands of dollars in his lifetime. When he died at the age of 68 years, he was penniless. He had been arrested 120 times and served more than ten years in prison as a result of 20 prison sentences. In one way or another, sin always leaves us bankrupt.

All of the brightness and joy went out of Ahab's new toy — Naboth's garden — when Elijah appeared. How could it ever bring him pleasure when Naboth's blood stained the ground? There is no deed which is purchased for sinful delights that does not come with an enormous price tag: including fear, guilt, bondage, and loss of peace.

51

There is no evil thing, no sin — large or small — which, if we know we are committing evil, will not later rise up to witness against us.

God does not (in this life) so much punish us *for* our sins as allows us to be punished *by* our sins.

A serious word of warning: If sin no longer troubles you, then you are in far more grave danger than you can imagine. You can stifle your conscience by continuing in wrong-doing until it no longer bothers you, and that cold, empty vacuum is a frightening thing to live with.

Sin is never worth the price you have to pay for it. It will indeed take you farther than you want to go and keep you longer than you want to stay!

Sin Blinds To True Friends

Sin is so blinding that we fail to recognize our sad situation. The story is told of two men who got into a very violent argument as to who had the sharper switch-blade knife. Finally, as words were not settling the issue, the knives under discussion were drawn and the fight was on in earnest. One man took a wild sweep at the other with a devastating arc of the blade. The other man jumped back and then jeered, "Ah ha! You missed!" Whereupon the first man said, "Yeah? Then try to shake your head!" So with sin. We can be dead in our sins and trespasses and never even know it.

Just so, sin blinds us as to who is enemy and who is a real friend. Ahab cried out, "Have you found me, O mine enemy?" "Enemy?" In truth, Elijah was the best friend Ahab had in the kingdom. Jezebel, the wife of his bosom, whom he loved and thanked for his new toy, was the worst enemy that hell could have sent him.

It is ever true. The one who loves enough to warn and rebuke is the truest friend of the sinner. The worst enemy any of us can have is the one who tempts us to sin, or who lulls us into thinking we are "not so bad," or "only human."

Sin always tries to place blame, preferably on someone or something else. A woman tells of returning from South Africa, and on a stop-over found herself in London's Heathrow Airport. She bought a cup of coffee and a small package of cookies, then with all of her carry-on luggage in hand, found an unoccupied table. She was engrossed in reading the morning paper when she became aware of a young man seated across the table from her, helping himself to her cookies. She didn't want to make a scene, so without saying anything she leaned over to take another cookie for herself. A minute or so passed and she heard more rustling of paper as the man helped himself to still another cookie. By this time they were down to the very last cookie in the package, and she was very angry, but still couldn't bring herself to say anything. Then the young man broke the last remaining cookie in two, pushed half across to her, ate the other half, and left. Sometime later when her flight was called, she was still fuming over the fellow's audacity. Imagine her embarrassment when she opened her purse to pull out her ticket and was confronted by her still-unopened package of cookies. All of the time she had been eating *his*! Sin does that, too. It always attempts to place the blame on another, rather than on oneself.

God sent a prophet named Nathan to King David. His sins seem so obvious to us: he seduced Bathsheba, another man's wife; committed adultery with her; and then arranged to murder her husband, Uriah. But it seemed not to trouble King David at all. But Nathan came telling the parable of the rich man. David's anger was kindled against the rich man and ordered that he should die. Courageously Nathan pointed his finger at the king and said, "Thou art the man!" Then David recognized his own guilt and knew, too, that Nathan, in pointing out his sin, was no enemy, but rather the man whom God had sent to open his eyes.

As a child when I insisted on doing something that was wrong, or not good for me, mother would forbid it. My immediate response to the discipline of her firm, "No," was to accuse, "You never want me to have any fun!" or "You don't love me or you'd let me do it!" Mother's standard reply was, "But I *do* love you. I just don't want you to be hurt, so I won't allow you to do it." That is no foe, but a loving parent of the best kind.

But how like Ahab we are. As sinners we stumble along in darkness and mistake the face of friend for foe. How good, actually, of God to give you a conscience to prick you — yet we call it an enemy. God sends chastisement or discipline or sorrows to draw us away from our sins, and we call them enemies. It is the unfailing love of God which will not leave us alone in our sinfulness. Paul said, "Do you not realize that God's kindness is meant to lead you to repentance?" (Romans 2:4b).

God gives us the gospel and a Bible with words of warning and judgment — and we turn from the book and its message and treat it as if it were an enemy.

God sends faithful preachers to declare that sin ends in death and we accuse the minister of bringing us terrible tidings. A girl in a beauty shop told me once, "I am a Christian, but I don't want to hear about the cross, or sin, or any of the bad things. Just give me the 'smiley stuff'!"

Elijah's words had often warned Ahab, and so he calls him "mine enemy." In the Garden of Eden the real enemy said, "Go ahead and disobey; go ahead and sin; eat the fruit; you shall not surely die." But the Bible says, "Be sure your sins will find you out." That is not the word of an enemy. Those are the words of the best Friend you will ever have!

Repent For Relief!

The message of Elijah to Ahab was a sentence of death for his crime against Naboth. Terrible judgment was promised him — but in fact it was given to lead the king to repentance.

Ahab partially repented and partially listened to Elijah's voice and God's warning — yet for all that he continued in his evil ways. So the merciful threat and warning became a stern prophecy which was fulfilled to the very letter.

Advertisers of a certain remedy for indigestion claim "Rolaids spell relief." God promises as a remedy for sin and its sure retribution that "repentance spells relief." Repentance is the godly sorrow for sin and a sincere turning from wrong-doing that guarantees God's forgiveness and mercy.

But to bring lasting relief, repentance must be true and sincere. God is not interested in our playing games with him. A Roman Catholic priest tells of a man who came to him in confession, saying, "Father, I have sinned." "What is your sin?" the priest inquired. The man responded, "Forgive me, Father, for last night I stole two bales of hay from my neighbor. No, you better make it three, for I plan to steal another one tonight." Such is not true repentance and God cannot and will not forgive those sins we have committed unless we are sorry enough to turn away from them in repentance and faith and not repeat them.

Not all seeming repentance is genuine. We may cry real tears and sound very sorry, but it is so easy to be fooled by appearances. I was scheduled to preach at the Virginia Annual Laity Conference. I called the home of Ward Jackson, the layman in charge of the event to make final arrangements. He was not at home, but his wife Diane assured me that he would be meeting me at the Richmond Airport upon my arrival. "How will I recognize him?" I asked. The wife said, "He will be wearing a big cowboy hat." I inquired further, "What if there is more than one man wearing a cowboy hat?" "Easy!" she said. "He'll be the best-looking man in the airport wearing a cowboy hat." When I disembarked at Richmond, I didn't see anyone at the gate who even remotely fit her description, so I went to the baggage claim area, thinking to find him there. No one was there that seemed to be Ward, so I collected my luggage, and then looked around, trying to decide my next course of action. Just then, some distance away, with his back to me, stood a tall, dark man wearing a cowboy hat. Sure that I had the right person, and remembering Diane's words, I walked over, tapped him on the shoulder, and before he turned said to him, "Excuse me, but are you the best-looking man in this airport wearing a cowboy hat?" He turned around, looked me over, and said, "Lady, it 'pears to me I'm the *only* man here with a cowboy hat!" — But it wasn't Ward Jackson! You and I can never judge by appearances the repentance of another. God alone looks on the heart and when he sees a sinner who is truly sorry for his/her sin, he is ready, willing, and anxious to forgive. The psalmist David, who was brought to repentance by the faithful prophet, Nathan, threw himself on the mercy of God and cried out, "A broken and a contrite heart thou wilt not despise" (Psalm 51:17). Luther said, "To sin no more is the highest repentance."

So when God's message comes to us, let us know that it is the concern of love and its gentle rebuke that is meant to save us from awful consequences and a heartbreaking judgment later.

A teacher in a Christian pre-school thought she would explain the basic concept of God to the children, and later asked them about it to see how much they understood. The topic that day was that God is eternal. She tried to be as simple with her explanation as possible, but when she later questioned them about what they had learned, one little girl eagerly raised her hand to say, "God is a turtle!" Well, God is eternal, *not* a turtle, and God is your friend, *not* your enemy, and God wants to forgive you, *not* punish you — but repentance is the key.

The preacher speaking God's truth is not your enemy. The Bible is not your enemy; the devil *is* your enemy! God only wants to break the bondage of your sin and stop your headlong rush to self-destruction and soul-suicide.

Jesus is the friend (not the enemy) of sinners. That is why they said of our Lord, "This man receiveth sinners and eateth with them." A woman named Edith, hearing this verse for the first time, thought they were calling her name specifically, but it could be any of us, or all. "This man receiveth sinners and *Edith* with them" — or Bill, or Barbara, or Sue, or Joe, or whatever your name is. The detractors of Jesus intended it as a deeply derogatory statement, but actually they gave him the highest of praise.

So Christ speaks to you today — and count yourself blessed indeed if, in this moment, your conscience is troubling you — for it means that Jesus the friend of sinners loves you and speaks to you and calls you from your sin and danger. He invites you to accept his gracious offer of pardon, forgiveness, and peace. He says, "I love you. Come, leave your sins and be free!"

The songwriter was right. Sin *will* take you farther than you want to go and keep you longer than you want to stay — but Jesus will forgive you more than you deserve and keep you with him as long as you'll stay!

Proper 7
Pentecost 5
Ordinary Time 12
1 Kings 19:1-4 (5-7) 8-15a

Deep Depression
Or High Hope?

Hope, for many, is as futile as the philosophy in a "Peanuts" comic strip which showed Linus and Charlie Brown leaning on a fence, talking. Linus says, "I guess it's wrong to be worrying about tomorrow, maybe we should think only about today." Charlie Brown interrupts him to say, "No, that's giving up. I'm still hoping that *yesterday* will get better!"

A lot of people have no hope for today, and are sure that tomorrow will be just as hopeless. Indeed, in our time "hope" has become a bad word. When the doctor calls us in to say of our sick loved one, "At least we can still hope," it doesn't seem to cheer us up, but rather depresses us. When we sigh, "Well, here's hoping," the message we give is that "I might as well give up." When we hear someone say, "Well, as long as there's life, there's hope," then we know it is *really* bad!

Hope has been devoured by hopelessness. You hear a lot of religious talk about faith and love, but hope is a seldom-used word. Once in a while you run into the exception. Presbyterian author and minister, David A. Redding, tells of their oldest Presbyterian elder who, at the age of 103, took out a three-year subscription to a magazine. And it turned out that his hope was not in vain, for the man lived to read the last issue of that subscription.

Many people, instead of being hopeful, are victims of hope-lessness. The current, modern word for this very real malady is depression, and depression is the common ailment of many Americans. There is, of course, the sickness of deep, extreme depression which calls for urgent, professional help. Some trag-ic examples are reported in the newspapers daily: a young, beautiful nurse, so afflicted with depression that she slashed her wrists a number of times, trying to kill herself; the girl who jumped off a bridge with her baby in her arms, depressed be-cause she feared she was not a good mother; a brilliant White House aide, ensnared by his own perfection, who took his own life; the student whose wife divorced him, who then went into depression, and managed to hang himself with the bed sheets in the maximum security ward of the hospital where he had been hospitalized. The cases are multitudinous, the causes are varied, the symptoms are different, but the bottom line is a hopelessness and depression that makes life unfit for living.

Psychiatrists say depression is the most common emotional problem in America. It has risen to epidemic proportions in the nation, and not one of us is immune. It is not a willful fault, nor is it a sin. It is a signal that something is wrong — we need *help* and we need *hope*! It is no disgrace. Some of the world's most sensitive people have been susceptible to depression. People like Beethoven, Tchaikovsky, Tolstoy, and Abraham Lincoln suffered form it. Two of the best preachers of this century, Harry Emerson Fosdick and J. Wallace Hamil-ton, fought depression. Winston Churchhill waged a lifelong battle against depression, which he called "my black dog." Even the great reformer, Martin Luther, got depressed. Once he said, "For more than a week I was close to the gates of death and hell. I trembled in all my members. Christ was wholly lost to me. I was shaken by desperation and blasphemy of God!"

The truth is, we all are depressed to some degree, at some time. Perhaps not to the extremes I have just mentioned, but we get to feeling low, useless, worthless, nervous, apathetic, no-account, worried, or just plain "blue." We call it having a "bad day." Dear Abby, in her column, listed some portents of a bad day: "You know it's going to be a rotten day when you wake up facedown on the pavement. You know it's going to be a bad day when your birthday cake collapses from the weight of the candles. You know it's not going to be a good day when you put both contact lenses in the same eye." Low days hit us all: even religious people, even Christians, even good, God-loving people, people like Elijah, the prophet of God in this scripture. God brought Elijah out of it, and by remembering the story we can learn how to be restored to health and the high spirits of hope.

Elijah, you recall, had that famous contest on Mount Carmel with the prophets of Baal. Each would build an altar for their god and then a sacrifice would be made. The god who answered by fire, consuming the sacrifice, would be declared *"the God*!" All day long the prophets of Baal prayed, without result, to their gods, but at eventide Elijah prayed his relatively short prayer and God answered by fire! What a high day it was for the prophet of God! His spirits were at an all-time high; he would never be "down" again! But it isn't many hours until Jezebel, the queen, is hard on his heels. She loved the prophets of Baal, and was angry at their defeat, and sent word to the prophet that she was out to get him, to kill him. Elijah reacted in fear and ran, ran a day's journey into the wilderness, sat down under a broom tree, and cried out to God in despair, "Let me die. I'm not better than my fathers, let me die." (You have felt that way, too. High and happy one day and the next low, blue, and strangely defeated.)

This lesson of Elijah gives us a valuable clue as to why we become depressed.

Reason For Depression

One reason for our depression is that sometimes we expect too much of ourselves. Elijah thought he was all alone, and that he was after all, not so important anyway. He said, "Let

61

me die. I'm not better than my fathers." We think we have failed God, or said the wrong thing, or that we don't matter to anyone. It is so easy to compare ourselves with others and then decide we are useless. And then, depression is often far removed from being rational, so for no apparent reason we are down.

Another cause for hopelessness is that we have examined the problem and decide we cannot solve it. This leads to worry, fatigue, and fear, so we succumb to despair. It happened to Elijah. He was afraid of Jezebel's threat and asked to be allowed to die. He was tired, sleepy, and exhausted. Fatigue and helplessness come easily to us in our frantic, everyday living. We have marital problems, money problems, children problems, parent problems, friend problems, lover problems, work problems, health problems, and the list goes on. We are afraid: afraid of failure, afraid of criticism, afraid of sickness, afraid of death, afraid of a thousand ghosts that haunt us daily. It seems as if something is always going wrong with our little world. No matter how good things seem for a while, there is always a "catch" to it. Dr. Paul Tournier recalls the remark his young son made one day. It was a rather philosophical comment. He said, "Everything's always okay, except for something."

Life does seem to be that way sometimes. There always seems to be "something" we would like to have different. As an African proverb puts it, "The trouble with finding ivory is that there is always an elephant attached to it."

You can't talk yourself out of depression, you can't reason yourself out of depression, and you can't be kidded out of depression. When its black fog settles in upon your spirit, you are debilitated by its very presence and power.

Remedy For Depression

This sermon is not an easy, do-it-yourself, easy-fix solution for depression. It is not an effort to over-simplify the problem, but rather to say that for some feelings of despair and hopelessness there are some practical remedies that *will* work.

We need to recognize, in advance, that some things will *not* effect a cure. Suicide provides no answer. And we have found that drugs are an absolute failure. They do not expand our consciousness; and tranquilizers, while sometimes helpful, do not give permanent peace. Frivolity and wishful thinking haven't worked. Telling someone to "cheer up" is an exercise in futility. I read a sign in a service station which said, "They said to me, 'Cheer up, things could be worse,' so I cheered up, and sure 'nough, things got worse!" Ignoring the problem and hoping it will go away has failed. This solution is reminiscent of the Arab who felt hungry one night. He lighted a candle, opened a date, and found it was wormy, so he threw it aside. He tried another, and it was wormy, too. A third and fourth had worms in them. So he blew out the candle and ate the fifth in the dark. Depression is real, frighteningly real to the person afflicted, so what is the remedy?

Remember, some depressions are so extreme they need the care of a trained doctor and perhaps medication. But for the depressions which settle in upon many of us, there are some tried antidotes that give real relief. These cures worked for Elijah, and perhaps they would work for you.

Elijah first did the sensible thing. He got some food and some rest. Remember the all-day contest on Mount Carmel? That must have left the prophet emotionally drained and the day's journey into the wilderness must have tried him almost to exhaustion. So, under the broom tree he said, "Let me die," and he fell down and went to sleep. It is amazing what a good night's sleep will do for a discouraged and cantankerous Christian. When he slept for a while, God woke him and fed him angel food cake. (I'm sure it was angel food cake. After all, it was cake brought by an angel, and in my wildest imaginings I can't think it was a devil's food cake.) Sometimes rest and food are all that are needed for a cure for despondency. It doesn't sound like the most "spiritual" of solutions, but

God used it to begin Elijah's journey back to confidence and hope.

The next thing Elijah did was to return to Horeb, to Sinai. He went back to the roots of his faith. It was there at Sinai that God had made a covenant with his people. In other words, he went back to his faith beginnings. Back to God — there is always solid hope in that action. The next thing you may need to do is to go back to the roots of your own Christian faith — back to God, back to church, back to the Bible. There you'll experience again what real hope is; it is that expectancy that God is there to help you in your present situation. The psalmist found that was his solution too. He cried out, "Why are you so downcast, O my soul? Why so disturbed within me? Put your hope in God, for I will yet praise him, my Savior and my God" (Psalm 43:5). It is expectantly waiting for the things from God that faith has already promised. As you worship, as you read the Word, as you pray, you will begin to realize how much God cares about you. You'll know you are not alone in your problem, that you are not fighting this battle by yourself. The first thing to do with your problem is to go to God, run to him, and be assured that he loves you, and understands your pain.

As you listen to him — when you pray and read the Bible — you will hear, as did Elijah, the still small voice of God. God has promised that "in quietness and confidence shall be your strength." God has said, "Be still and know." Far too often we "rush around and guess." The story is told of two brothers; one was 16 years old, the other only about nine. The older brother never wanted to tell the younger boy anything of his private business, so he was especially secretive when it came to courting his first girlfriend. He had gone with the girl for several weeks, and was trying to work up the nerve to kiss her. One night he planned his evening carefully, and at the proper time he took his girl by the arm, walked casually out to the back yard, clear beyond the back fence, to an old cottonwood tree. He sat down with her under the tree. He had no idea that his kid brother had climbed the tree earlier, and now sat among the branches, seeing and hearing everything that went on. Finally, the older boy bolstered his nerve, lifted his eyes to the sky as if he were praying, and said, "Heavenly Father, up above, may I kiss the girl I love?" Immediately he was answered by a voice from the treetops which said, "Sixteen-year-old down below, pucker up and let 'er go!"

But the certainty of God's voice coming to us is no childish prank. He does come to us, he does speak to us . . . sometimes through a sermon, or a prayer, maybe in the voice or actions of a friend, perhaps a portion of the scriptures, or even in the stirrings of your conscience. When he comes, your first reaction may be of guilt for your sins. This awakening to your own sinfulness may for a time only increase the depression, but if you face them, confess them, and accept the forgiveness of God, you will be amazed that as God forgives you and you forgive yourself that high hopes will once again be born in you.

Perhaps the last thing that Elijah did was to offer the unconditional surrender of himself to God. God told the prophet to "go — and anoint Elisha in his place." This could not have been easy. It took real surrender to step aside and allow another to take his place. But Elijah did it. No wonder Elijah had been depressed. He had been thinking of himself for far too long. That will get you to feeling despondent every time. Elijah had told God, "*I* have been doing your will, I, I am the only one left." Forget yourself and lose yourself in God! We never know real Christian hope and joy until we surrender unconditionally to our Lord. God's forgiveness and friendship is the only fun that really lasts. Life lived for God is step by step, day by day, moment by moment. Hope is not for the major crises of your life. It is what gets you there a day at a time, but that hope only comes from living in the center of the will of God. A dean at Princeton University said one of his boys found a record of a Beethoven sonata, bored a hole about a half-inch off-center, and played the record from the hole. It was the same record, but the music sounded like the cackling of a thousand Walt Disney witches. A life that is not God-centered, God-surrendered, and God-focused won't make music, only noise.

Get High Hopes From Jesus!

Elijah started out so depressed he wanted to die, but when we last see him, the Record says, "And Elijah went by a whirlwind into heaven" (2 Kings 2:11). Instead of death, Elijah got a translation. Talk about an all-time high! Like Enoch, he never did die; he was taken to heaven alive. Such is the hope of the Christian. Jesus said, "He that liveth and believeth in me shall never die." Phillips Brooks said, "The great Easter truth is not that we are to live newly after death — that is not the great thing — but that we are to be new here and now by the power of the resurrection!"

Transporting a person from depression to high spirits is a triumph of hope. Everything does not have to go well for us to have high hopes if we belong to Christ. Even on the cross Jesus endured the shame and agony of it for the best of reasons: "the *joy* that was set before him."

Christ has the cure for your depression, for your hopelessness, for your despair. He wants to give you radiant joy and high hope. No other religion does what Christ does. However high the marks we may give other world religions, none of them score very high on joy and hope. Buddhism recommends the philosophical equivalent of slow suicide. Hinduism is too vague to be very joyful. Islam is too fierce to find anything very amusing. But the Westminster Catechism spells it out for the Christian faith when it says, "The chief end of man is to glorify God and to *enjoy* him forever." That's not so depressing, is it? In fact, that's a strong reason for hope!

Life's
Final Flight

Some of the largest ads in newspapers, and some of the best commercials on television, deal with flying. Some people think that flying is "the only way to go," others fly only because they must and "white-knuckle" it all the way, and some simply refuse to fly at all, claiming that "if God intended us to fly he would have given us wings."

Some delightful stories come out of airplane experiences. One such tale deals with the time when the passengers in a large jet plane were already anxious because of bad weather, then the ride became rough, and then much rougher. When their anxiety was at a very high peak, the voice of the pilot came over the public address system saying, "Ladies and gentlemen, this is your pilot. If you will look out the left windows you will notice a large crack in the left wing that is getting worse by the minute. Then if you who are on the right side will look out those windows, you will note that one engine is smoking and the other one is on fire. If you could see the rear of the plane, you'd know that the tail assembly is about to fall off. Now look just below you, and you will see several parachutes. Ladies and gentlemen, that is your crew. This is a recording, recording, recor ...."

Then there is the story of the pilot who told his passengers, "I have some good news and some bad news. The bad news is that we are lost. The good news is that we are making very good time." And so the stories abound, no doubt because we Americans fly the skies a lot, and we never tire of a good anecdote. But whether you fly or not, and regardless of how you feel about it, there is still one flight that each of us *must* take. That is the flight that takes us from death into life, from earth to heaven, from time to eternity.

Obviously there is nothing in the scriptures that has to do with jet planes, but it is amazing how parallel to airplane flight is the flight of the soul when it goes to meet God. Let us use Elijah's translation as a parable of that experience. Probably the closest thing to flight that we have in the Bible is Elijah's translation to heaven. God accomplished it so he didn't even have to die or be buried. God sent horses and a chariot of fire for Elijah and took him to heaven in a whirlwind. Let us use this story as a parabolic narrative to remind us of how our flight will be. The chariot and horses will be an airplane, and the whirlwind will be the air that bears us aloft. At death, our soul takes its flight to its eternal home and destiny. The time of our death is strikingly similar to a final airplane flight.

The Time Of Departure

It is no problem at all in an airport terminal to find the time of your flight departure. It will be flashed on a television screen, a friendly company employee will give you the information, it is written on your ticket, and it is relayed over the public address system. If you want to know when you are leaving, you can easily find out.

But no one knows for sure when his/her flight will be taken from earth to heaven. Death is unexpected even when we expect it. It often comes suddenly, unannounced, and sometimes prematurely. A Prudential Insurance commercial shows a man on an escalator, ascending to heaven, saying, "Somehow I thought I'd have more time." But death is a fact of life. This is evidenced by the fact that there are some 26,000 funeral homes in America, and during any one year they will do several billion dollars in burial business. This is because approximately two million Americans die yearly. That means about 5,479 people each day, 228 each hour, and as you read these figures some four persons have gone to meet God.

Some people refuse to think about death or talk about it. We even avoid the word itself, substituting other words or phrases for death and dying. We say "he passed on," "expired," "fell asleep," "made the exit," "gave up the ghost," "was called home," and other such analogies. Some expressions are less sensitive, even crude, as they make the point: "He went west, "he kicked the bucket," "he hopped the twig," "he bit the bullet," "he bought the farm." We will say almost anything to avoid simply saying "dying" or "dead."

A seminary professor gave a real word of wisdom as he taught a class on death to his students, saying, "Until we accept our own mortality we are not ready to face life."

A Florida newspaper tells of a cemetery in that state where stands a tiny masonry building. In it is a casket containing a body that has never been buried. The dead woman's husband used to come to that building every day. He surrounded the casket with items she had loved. Neon lights flashed over the door. He would invite passersby to come in for a chat. He would throw parties in the little building on her birthday and on other special occasions. Then the husband died and was buried in another state. Now the little building stands forlornly in its corner, lights off, door locked, still housing the body of a woman greatly loved, but sadly testifying to the fact that one man could not face the reality of death. But we had better learn to face the reality, for our departure time may be announced at any hour. Listen to the news on television and read the headlines and obituaries of almost any newspaper and you will know how uncertain and unexpected the hour of our parting may be. It is no accident that God's Word enjoins us to be ready. God, through Amos the prophet, says, "Prepare to meet thy God," and the psalmist says, "Teach us to number our days."

The Ticket

No one is allowed on a plane without a ticket. It may be a special fare ticket, a coach or first class ticket, a tour-group rate ticket, or a stand-by ticket, but you must have a ticket. They are usually purchased in advance. You pay for it with cash or a credit card. It is not valid until it has been paid for.

We need a ticket, too, for our own final flight. Last minute purchases of a ticket for the flight of the soul seldom work out too well. If you wait until you are dying, it could be too late. There is but one deathbed repentance in the Bible: that of the dying thief on the cross who asked to be remembered by Jesus when he came into his kingdom. Only one recorded: perhaps that none of us may presume on last minute ticket purchasing, but still there is one, so that no one need despair. It is far safer to buy your ticket in advance. Jesus Christ has provided a ticket for all who believe in him. He purchased it with his own blood. It is stamped "paid in full," paid by the red blood of his body as he hung on the cross. No wonder we sing, "Jesus paid it all, All to him I owe; sin had left a crimson stain, He washed it white as snow." No person ever paid so much for a ticket for another.

The Baggage

You can only take on board with you the baggage that will fit under your seat or in the overhead compartment. The rest has to be checked and stowed in the luggage hold of the plane. This can be a real headache. You may get to your destination and have to wait and wait and wait to claim your baggage. But worse than the wait, occasionally you find your luggage has not arrived with you at all.

Your luggage for heaven is handled differently. You have heard the old adages: "There are no pockets in a shroud," and "You can't take it with you." The story is told of a man who knew he was facing death in the near future, and he said to three of his friends, "I know they say you can't take it with you, but I'd sure like to try. I'm entrusting $30,000 to each of you. When I die, pass by my casket at the funeral service, and each of you put that money in my hands." They solemnly promised to do as he asked. He did die a short time later and after the funeral his three friends met for coffee to talk over the good times they had shared with their now deceased buddy. Finally, one of them, the preacher, said, "My conscience is really bothering me, and I must confess to you what I have done. I really needed $10,000 to finish out our mission program in the church, so I took it from our friend's money, and only put $20,000 in his hand." The second man, a doctor, said, "Well, I have a confession to make, too. I needed some special equipment that I thought would help a lot in treating my patients, so I held back $20,000 and only put $10,000 in my buddy's hands." The lawyer said, "You really disappoint me. Since our pal trusted me with his money, I tell you what I did. As I passed by, I put a check in his hands for the full $30,000!" But it is no joke that heaven's luggage must be sent on ahead. There is no use in heaven for material things at all: money, clothes, cosmetics, shoes, and hair dryers you don't need. Spiritual baggage is what you want to pack for your flight to heaven. Jesus said, "Lay not up for yourselves treasures on earth, but in heaven where thieves do not break in and steal, where moth and rust do not corrupt."

So we send our good works to heaven ahead of us. God saves us, and it is grace and grace alone that provides our ticket. The purchase price was paid by the blood of Jesus, but our works do follow after us. You need never worry about who gets the credit for all the good you do on earth. God keeps good records, and it will be reward time for us later.

The Destination

You can take a plane to almost anywhere in the world: Frankfort, London, Moscow, Tokyo, Honolulu, Paris or wherever. Sometimes you must change planes, sometimes it will be a nonstop flight. But, in every case, death is a single, nonstop flight. There are no round-trip tickets. Reincarnation is a sick joke of an unbelieving world who would rather not remember that "it is appointed unto man *once* to die, and after that the judgment." There is no intermediate place where you can change your mind about your destination, you can't make a new decision enroute. It is in this life, and this life only, where our decision is made to be saved or lost. In the southeast, we have a saying, "You can't go to heaven or hell without changing planes in Atlanta." The truth is, when you leave on this final flight, there is no stopping in Atlanta, or any place else. If you have a ticket, paid for by Jesus, you go straight to heaven!

A Christian never needs to be concerned about winding up at the wrong destination. You can be sure, now, of heaven. One of the early heroes and martyrs of the Christian Church was Justin of Nablus in Palestine. A philosopher and a lover of wisdom, he was one day captured by Christ. He became a preacher of the gospel for 35 years, until he was caught and imprisoned in Rome for his faith. At his trial, a judge asked him, "Listen, you who are before me. Are you a Christian?" "Yes, I am a Christian," replied Justin. "Then," sneered the judge, "listen, you who are called learned and wise and think you know the truth. If you are scourged and beheaded, do you suppose that you will go to heaven?" "I not only suppose it," he replied, "I *know* it!" Never doubt it, if you believe in Christ as Savior, you are going to heaven, too!

The Plane

On your final flight, your plane may be a DC 1011, a 747, a 727, or a Piper Comanche or a Beechcraft or Cessna — it may be a small or enormous plane. All these planes will get you to your destination if they are in good condition and properly flown. For the soul, the church is the plane which gets us to heaven. Never underestimate the value of the church in your life. Luther said, "He that would find Christ must first find the church, for outside the church there is no Christ, no truth, and no salvation." Paul Loeffler once wrote, "To be a Christian without the church is to decapitate the head from the body."

A lady in Fayetteville, Georgia, once told me: "I am 84 years old. All of my life I have been in the church. I've had many joys and many sorrows, and I could not have lived without the church." A little white church on the sea coast of Great Britain was destroyed by a storm. The congregation was poor and decided that they could never raise enough money to rebuild it, so they began looking for someplace else to meet. A few days later an official from the Admiralty came to see them. When they told him their problem he said, "If you cannot afford to rebuild, then we will do it for you. You see, that church spire has become a landmark by which the ships of the seven seas steer their courses. It is on all the charts and maps. We would dash to pieces on the reefs if we could not steer by the steeple. We cannot be without it!" We can never emphasize enough the importance of the church. The church does not have as many proponents in our day as it once had, but that does not diminish its value. It is the lighthouse that draws us to Christ the Light of the world; it is what points our way to heaven. It is the keeper of the charts that guides us there. It is the inspirer of our faith, the keeper of the keys to the kingdom.

Just as all planes are different, so many churches are diverse. There are small rural churches with perhaps only a few members, and mega-churches with thousands of members. Some are Lutheran, others United Methodist, Presbyterian, Catholic, Eastern Orthodox, or Baptist. As long as they proclaim Christ as the way to God and heaven, they all fly! But never trust a plane or a church that promises a safe arrival on heaven's shores if they are using the wrong map. If they use any chart other than the holy scriptures, find another plane!

73

The Pilot

The big questions in every safe flight are: "Who is the pilot? How competent is he? Does he know the way? Is he trustworthy? Is he skilled?" Jesus Christ is the ticket, he is the head of the plane (the church), and he is the pilot who gets us safely there.

Once, as I was learning to fly a small plane, I was out practicing some solo takeoffs and landings. As I was coming in to land on the runway, everything was in order, the glide was properly established, the engine's RPMs were about right, when suddenly I noticed that the windsock had changed direction and was now blowing 180 degrees in the other direction. This meant I had to climb out, establish a new pattern, land north instead of south, and start the whole procedure all over again. I did this, and then found just as I was ready to land, the wind had shifted once more. This happened three or four times and I was about to panic, thinking I'd never get that little J-3 Cub on the ground safely. I had no idea what to do, since the wind wouldn't stand still for me, but then I saw my instructor standing on the end of the runway. His white shirt sleeves showed up clearly as he pointed the direction for me to land, regardless of what that fluctuating wind-sock said. So, when the terrors of death would grab hold of us, we can relax in perfect safety and peace, knowing our Divine Instructor is pointing the way — not with a white-sleeved shirt, but with a nail-scarred hand, saying, "I am the Way, the Truth, and the Life." No one ever trusted this Divine Pilot without coming in for a safe landing in heaven's holy harbor.

Elijah went up by a whirlwind to heaven. We will one day go by faith in Christ to that happy shore where our loved ones and Jesus wait!

Naaman
Is My Name!

Some of the most profound precepts we ever know come clothed in very basic and elemental forms. A "Peanuts" cartoon strip shows Charlie Brown visiting Lucy who is at her stand offering psychiatric help for a nickel. Charlie says, "I need help! Tell me a great truth. Tell me something about living that will help me." Lucy responds by asking, "Do you ever wake up at night and want a drink of water?" "Sure," Charlie responds, "quite often." Lucy then offers her advice, "When you're getting a drink of water in the dark, always rinse out the glass because there might be a bug in it! Five cents, please." Charlie pays, and walks away saying, "Great truths are even more simple than I thought they were."

Another illustration of this is a mother telling of overhearing a conversation between her two daughters. The younger one had been having considerable frustration trying to learn how to know which shoe went on which foot. "Listen," said the older girl to the younger, "I'm going to tell you something and I want you to remember this the rest of your life. Do you *promise* to remember this for as long as you live?" The younger girl meekly promised, "Yes." The older sister said, "Okay, here it is. Whenever you put on your shoe, if it hurts, you've got it on the wrong foot!"

The lesson in this text is like that: profound and deep, but simple, basic, and easy to understand. Look at this man named Naaman, who is so much like ourselves that we could easily say, "Naaman is also my name!"

The Condition

Naaman was a great man, a valiant soldier, commander of the Syrian army, highly regarded, "but he was a leper." Have you ever noticed how life could often be perfect, except for the "buts"?

Naaman had leprosy. We don't know how he got it, but we do know that in his time it was symbolic of God's displeasure. We also know there was no cure for it. The rule was simple: "You have leprosy, you die!"

In our time we have a modern-day leprosy: AIDS. We know some of the ways you can get the virus. One prominent athlete brags of having 20,000 different sexual partners. The media report that Magic Johnson admits to getting the HIV virus through his own promiscuity. Some are infected with the virus through inoculating themselves with drugs, using dirty needles. Some who are infected are completely innocent: like the late Arthur Ashe who was infected from a bad blood transfusion. Some innocent wives are infected by their husbands, or an innocent baby gets the virus from the mother's blood which carries into her unborn child. But, innocent or guilty, again the axiom is tragically simple: "You have AIDS, you die an early death."

Not all persons in Naaman's day had leprosy, nor do all in our day have AIDS. But there *is* a deadly disease to which we have all been exposed. It has infected the whole human race, and it rages like a virulent, lethal fever in us all. We are sick, sick, sick, with *sin*! We took that terrible fall in the Garden of Eden and have been infected ever since. There is no man-made cure, and no exceptions, and no doubt as to the outcome. Again the rule is simple: "You sin, you die!"

76

But, oh, how we hate to admit to the malady. Instead of seeking a cure, we've tried to redefine the illness. We've tried to neutralize the seriousness of the disease by using soft-terms. So, we no longer steal, we borrow or confiscate. We seldom refer to fornication, but call it, instead, premarital sex — it sounds so much better. No one commits adultery, we just have extramarital sex. The practice of homosexuality is not perversion, but rather an alternate lifestyle. Dirty movies are not for dirty-minded people, but for mature audiences. Sin is not sin, but rather human error, a simple mistake, or bad judgment. We've assumed that if we can define sin to a more tasteful word, maybe it won't be so bad and God won't condemn us for it.

But words cannot change the reality itself! God views these efforts to downplay our actions with words by saying, "Woe unto them that call evil good, and good evil; that put darkness for light, and light for darkness; that put bitter for sweet, and sweet for bitter" (Isaiah 5:20).

But, a sinner by any other name is just as lost! No wonder Seneca said, "Sin is the 'universal insanity.'" We may not have leprosy, we may have escaped AIDS, but we *are* sick in our sins!

> *The worst of all diseases is light compared with sin,*
> *On every side it seizes, but rages most within;*
> *It's palsy, plague, and fever, and madness all combined,*
> *And none but a believer the least relief can find.*

Our name *is* Naaman — and what a mess we are in!

The Command

Through the witness of a young girl in Samaria, whose name we do not know, Naaman finally winds up being sent to the prophet of God named Elisha. Naaman pulls up to Elisha's door with his full retinue of servants and horses and

77

chariots, ready to grace the prophet with his impressive presence (leper though he was), but — surprise — the prophet doesn't even bother coming to the door! Elisha didn't come out to greet him, or have him sign the visitor's register, or stand and tell him his name, or how honored he was by his visit. Elisha sent a servant out with a message — a simple, almost insulting message: "Go wash — dip seven times in Jordan, and you will be cured."

And did that ever upset Naaman! He was furious! "Behold, I thought ...." Just like ourselves, wasn't he? We always thought we could figure it out for ourselves. But we can't, for God has already told us, "My thoughts are not your thoughts, nor my ways your ways, for as the heavens are higher than the earth, so are my thoughts than your thoughts, and my ways than your ways" (Isaiah 55:8).

Naaman, ranting and raving and raging says, "I thought the prophet himself would come out to see me and pray for me. I don't like the treatment nor the remedy — besides, there are, in my country, bigger and better and cleaner rivers than the muddy Jordan. Back home we have the Abana and Pharbar rivers and they are much nicer"; so Naaman went huffing off in an irate rage.

The spirit of Naaman inhabits us all. We have become a nation of syncretists. We take a little of this religion and a little of that and make our own "brand." So we try to meld together from Christianity the philosophy of Jesus with his teaching on love and compassion. From Eastern religions we borrow ideas related to the thought that each person can be his/her own god. This is where the New Age movement gets much of its impetus. Then we take a bit from something else and finally have our "mix-and-match" combination that we call our "personal faith." But, have you ever noticed how much easier it is to spend a dozen hours discussing religion than a half hour obeying God? We often content ourselves with a merely friendly and appealing Jesus, instead of a strong, imperial, commanding Lord. We dote on a gospel of good fellowship and camaraderie, instead of a gospel of downright obedience. Perhaps we would do well to remember that Christ does not court any man or woman, but *commands* us! Again, the rule is pretty simple: "Ye must be born again! Repent and believe the gospel!"

But Naaman was blessed by having some pretty sane and sensible servants who reminded him, "If the prophet had told you to do something great, or hard, you wouldn't have had any trouble with that. You would have been glad to tackle a hard assignment, but don't forget, you *are* a leper. You *are* dying. Maybe your pride is not all that important. Maybe you ought to at least try what the prophet says. You can't be your own doctor anymore."

Yes, our name *is* Naaman! We are so much like him, and on our best days we admit that our worst inclination is to sin, that we are sick with it, that it is incurable, and we are dying.

Admitting to sin is far better than excusing ourselves. Jeffrey Holland, former president of Brigham Young University said, "One lament I cannot abide is the poor, pitiful, withered cry, 'Well, that's just the way I am.' Spare me your speeches. I've heard them from too many people who wanted to sin and call it psychology."

We sinning humans keep trying something else other than the simple, humble formula of coming to God through repentance and faith in Jesus Christ. Like Naaman, we say, "I thought" — but our ideas are as useless as his. We entertain ideas like the New Age movement which suggests we pray to the God inside of us, or the God all around us, or to the trees, or whatever, and then we'll like ourselves more and feel lots better. Or another idea: "God is too good and loving to let me die. He didn't really mean that 'the wages of sin is death.' " Or another thought: "Maybe we can make enough brownie points with our good works and clean living that God will forget about our sins." Like Naaman, we become upset that God would ask us to "wash in the Jordan." We think we cannot admit we have sinned, that we can't make it on our own.

The Cure

But, once we stop insisting on "our way," then there is hope that we can accept God's cure. As soon as we admit we are dying, as soon as we concede the battle, then there is hope for us. Naaman must wash in the Jordan, there was no other remedy. God is just as adamant that our excuses and substitutes are unacceptable, and that we submit to his remedy.

In Wagner's comic strip, "Grin and Bear It," two ladies are sitting in the doctor's waiting room. One says, "I'm still looking for a second opinion. The last five doctors I have been to have all told me the same thing." So when sin is diagnosed as our condition, we need not look for a second opinion. We need, instead, to go to God's grace for forgiveness. There is no other cure!

The cross, and Christ's death upon it, were far too costly to negate by replacing it with something that is "more pleasant." A woman in my church once asked me to stop using the song, "There Is A Fountain Filled With Blood." "I'd like something a little nicer and more refined," she said. "Something that is not so repugnant." How ridiculous! We tolerate a violent society on television and in actuality on our streets and in our homes, and yet won't accept a suffering Savior dying in our place on a cross because it is repugnant! The cross must have been an offense to Jesus too, for in the Garden of Gethsemane he prayed, "Father, if it is possible, let this cup pass — if there is another way, let me by-pass the cross." But even Jesus could not sidestep its agony, for without the cross there is no cure!

We will never find a way to reduce the harsh judgment of God upon all human sin that the cross represents. A blood-stained, nail-pierced, splintered, rough-hewn cross-tree is an ugly thing, and no matter how we sentimentalize it, or call it foolishness and weakness and offensive, it still is the only cure for the curse of sin that holds us fast in its ugly grip.

Think about a person lying in a hospital, dying for lack of blood, and then a life-giving transfusion is received and the patient is made to feel like new again. That is exactly what the cross does. The life-giving blood, flowing from the riven side of the Redeemer gives us life for our death, hope for our despair, and salvation for our lostness. Christ, by his cross, changes our past, our present, and our future.

Let it be clearly understood by anyone who would embrace Christianity that at its very heart and center is the cross! Our sin-cure was effected at Calvary, not in Bethlehem; not in Nazareth, but on Golgotha. The cross is not a symbol, it is an *act*. But never forget that the gospel of the cross is always two-edged. It speaks of grace, but it brings judgment upon those who refuse that grace. How right the songwriter who penned these lines was:

> *I must needs go home by the way of the cross,*
> *There's NO OTHER WAY but this,*
> *I shall ne'er get sight of the gates of light,*
> *If the way of the cross I miss.*
> *The way of the cross leads home . . .*

So, like the prodigal son who came to his senses, and returned to the waiting Father, so Naaman came to his senses, went and dipped, and wonder of wonders, he came clean! The ugly rotting flesh of Naaman was restored like that of a young child. You've noticed the perfection of a baby's skin: without acne, without age wrinkles, without blemish. So perfect was Naaman's cure! That is what happens when you obey God and plunge into the crimson flood of Calvary's suffering Savior's blood — *you come clean!*

The Land Of Beginning Again

Being cured by meeting the conditions of God is like entering into the land of beginning again. As soon as Naaman was cured, he wanted to pay. But Elisha refused any kind of payment, teaching us that we can never buy our salvation. Of course you will want to spend the rest of your life finding ways of expressing your gratitude to God for what he has done for you, but you can't pay for it!

Naaman asked to take some earth back to his own land. He knew he was going back to a heathen land where Elisha's and Israel's God was not served, but to Naaman this place where he found his healing would always be "holy ground." He felt he just had to have some dirt from the place where he found the cure. Again, he is not too different from us. We've long since learned that the church pointed us to Christ. But though you can't live your life at church, you *can* take some of the experience back into the world from whence you came. You can take Christ where you live, where you work, where you play. Like Naaman, take as much of the "holy ground" as possible because you just may be the person God uses to bring a soul-cure to another sin-sick person. There's a whole world out there looking for the land of beginning again!

Unusual, To
Say The Least!

When I was a 19-year-old kid-preacher, I was trying to preach my first revival in a small, north Missouri town. It was an eight-day revival, and I had literally worked for months trying to get the ten required sermons together. God had wonderfully blessed the series, crowds came (perhaps because there was nothing else much doing in the town and also because they had never seen a 19-year-old preacher, particularly of the "girl" type), decisions were made for Christ, and a lot of people were inspired. The pastor asked, then, that the revival continue for the second week. That was fine, but I told him I had already preached all the sermons I had (and, I suspected, all the sermons there WERE in the Bible), but I consented to stay on. I committed myself to the second week because the pastor blithely promised me, "Open your mouth, Barbara, and the Lord will fill it." That may be fine when you are standing before magistrates, but don't ever try it in the pulpit for revivals! I all but sweat blood trying to find something to say. The truth is, I had probably already told them all I knew in the first two nights I was there. But, desperately hunting for a text for the evening message, I happened upon Amos — Amos 4:12 — "Prepare to meet Thy God, O Israel." With a lot of naivete, brashness, ignorance, and much eisegesis, I preached a fierce, judgment day message. The sermon was bad, the August

83

night was hot, the windows had no screens, the bugs flew inside in droves, I swallowed some of them, and then, to further compound the already pitiful situation I was in, a cat came down the center aisle of the church, up to the pulpit, and rubbed against my legs. A "pillar" of the church came and took it from me and dropped it out an open window, and the floundering sermon continued. But the cat came back! I decided to let it alone and when it settled down behind me I breathed a sigh of relief. Then, I forgot about it, stepped back on it, and it yelped and scratched, in anger and fury, at being treated so shabbily in church. The same man put it out the same window, the crowd roared with laughter, and I closed the service. From that day until this — right now — I have never tried to preach from Amos again!

The truth is, this unusual book should not be taken lightly. Its lessons are as relevant as your next breath. Here is a man from a small town about six miles south of Bethlehem and 11 miles from Jerusalem. Almost everything about him is ordinary, until God takes over, and then some unusual events take place. The story of Amos is the story of every man and woman when God comes into the picture.

An Unlikely Prophet

Amos was from a little town in Judah called Tekoa. He earned his living taking care of sheep and the sycamore grove. Because of his skill with words and the strikingly broad range of his general knowledge of history and his world, we realize that he was not an ignorant peasant.

Even though he made his home in the southern kingdom, God called him to announce his judgment on the northern kingdom of Israel. By his own witness, which he made in defending his right to be a prophet to the angry Amaziah, he was neither a paid prophet nor a prophet's son. He was simply a shepherd and a man who cultivated sycamore-fig trees. "But the Lord took me from tending the flock," he said, "and God called me to 'go, prophesy to my people Israel.' "

A more unlikely prophet could scarcely be found. He went from the farm where he talked with the animals and dressed the trees, to proclaim to a nation, including its king, that they needed to mend their ways. His call and his credentials were not from any connection with the professional prophets, but from God alone.

God still chooses to call some very unlikely persons into his service. I, personally, am far from being a shining star as a preacher, but the fact that I do it at all is unusual, to say the least. I was called into the ministry as a teenager. I had never even heard of a woman preacher when I answered God's call upon my life. I came from a family poor in material possessions; I was introverted, insecure, and painfully shy. The fact that I am still in the ministry (less than 100 years later) is something of a miracle in itself.

And how about you? Did you ever once think you would one day sing in the choir, that you would teach a Sunday school class, that you would lead a women's or men's group, or sit on a church board and be a part of a decision making group for the whole church? Did you ever dream, before you came to Christ, that you would be one who fearlessly witnessed for him and tried to live your life as he directed? You were an unlikely candidate as well, huh? But one day, while you were "tending sheep and dressing trees" (or selling insurance, or managing a company, or digging a ditch, or building a house, or performing heart surgery, or pleading a court case, or whatever), God called you, and however unlikely it seemed, the glad result is that here you are doing exactly what God called you to do. Unusual, to say the least, isn't it?

The truth is that fundamental qualities for ministry are within reach of every consecrated person. It is not required that one be a person of unusual intellectual ability. What is demanded is virtue that is sweetened by the spirit of Jesus Christ. The spiritualization of our average capacities is much more important than the possession of unusual powers. Our ordinary abilities, when touched by the Spirit of God, become extraordinary.

An Unpopular Preacher

There is no guarantee that when God takes you in hand for his purposes that everything will automatically go smoothly and well.

Amos saw that both Judah and Israel were enjoying great prosperity. They had reached the heights in political power and military might. But both kingdoms were corrupt to the core. Idolatry was rampant, there was extravagant indulgence in luxurious living, immorality, corruption, and terrible oppression of the poor. Amos came on the scene sounding out God's displeasure at the utterly rotten social state of the nation, and then he issued a clarion call to repent and practice justice.

At first, they sort of liked Amos. He began by preaching against rival nations. He lashed out at their deeds and spelled their doom. It was sort of like today when the preacher berates the murderers, condemns the communists, castigates thieves, rebukes the practice of incest, and upbraids the drug pushers. You can get a lot of affirmation when you preach that way, when you "let the other, really bad guys, have it." So, at first, there was total agreement with Amos, for they were delighted when the promises of wrath were falling on "somebody worse than we are." Then, just when he had his hearers lulled into sweet, self-righteous satisfaction, Amos came to the punch line of his sermon and denounced *them* for social injustice.

A recent cartoon shows a couple leaving the church after worship, with the man saying to the minister at the door, "I liked your sermon — except for the parts that made me feel guilty." We never like the preacher too much when he begins to make us feel uncomfortable.

A timid minister, who often straddled the fence, was told by one member of his congregation to preach the "old-fashioned gospel," and was instructed by another to be "broad-minded." The result of his struggle was evident the next time he preached. He said, "Unless you repent, in a measure, and are converted, so to speak, you are, I am sorry to say, in danger of hell-fire and damnation, to a certain extent." But Amos was no fence-straddler, he came speaking a "thus saith the Lord," and was soon out of favor with his hearers. And they decided he had to go! Amaziah invited him to leave, to go back go Judah and tell his message to them.

Preaching of God's displeasure with our sins and of his impending judgments upon our lives of disobedience is no more popular today than it was a long time ago. If Amos' oracles are to mean anything to us, we must realize that it is just a single giant step from this 8th century prophet of the Old Testament to the modern 20th century. The lessons are the same. God still governs nations and individuals and ultimately no national sin and no personal sin goes unnoticed or unpunished.

This kind of preaching got Amos in trouble, and it got Jesus in trouble, too. Jesus was not crucified for saying, "In my Father's house are many mansions," or "Consider the lilies of the field," or "Lo, I am with you alway," or "Love one another." They did not nail Jesus to a cross because he went about doing good. He was nailed to the tree because two nations, one great and one small, Rome and Israel, were absolutely scandalized by his vision of a kingdom different from anything either of them had ever dreamed.

When Jesus began his first sermon in Nazareth, they liked the message for a while. They might have even been proud of their "local-hometown boy making good." How pleased they were to hear that he had come to "recover the sight of the blind," to "deliver the captives," and "release the oppressed." But as he continued, they got so upset with him they wanted to run him out of town. When he told the congregation that God is not a simple, local, tribal deity, that was not the sermon they wanted. They wanted God to bring down wrath on "other" nations. They were mad at the preacher and even tried to throw him over a cliff. Of course, we don't treat preachers that way today. We just stop going to church, ignore the sermon, quit paying tithes, and tell the folks at the Sunday dinner table that "this preacher is sure not as good as the last one we had!"

Preachers are not the only witnesses for Christ who can be unpopular and in disfavor with others. Many of the fine laity could tell of experiences where friends don't mind their talking about the joy and peace and love of Jesus, but they'd like them to stay away from conversation that deals with God's severe displeasure at our specific sins. How many Christians have found themselves out of favor with the boss because they refused to lie or they refused to compromise their principles on the poor ethics of a business deal? Many have found that they are not considered really "in," because they do not tolerate filthy innuendoes or refuse to laugh at racist remarks.

I said to a man in a church I pastored, "You are glad for me to be your pastor. You call me to bury your dead, you want me to baptize your babies, you ask me to counsel your wife and friends, but you never invite me to your parties. Why is that?" His quiet response was, "Oh Preacher, you really wouldn't want to come. But I don't invite you for two reasons. One, you wouldn't approve of what goes on, and two, your presence would be a real wet-blanket to the activities we have planned." Unpopular is what the Christian becomes in a world that is given over to lust, deceit, and decadence!

The Unbelievable Promise

God's imminent judgment on Israel for her sins was not to be a mere slap on the wrist to warn them, as he often had before, but it was the ominous word of an almost total destruction of the nation. The unthinkable was about to come to pass. God would uproot his people for their sins and lack of repentance, and he would do it by the hands of a pagan nation.

But still — even so — unbelievable as it seemed — *if* they would repent, God would still have mercy on the remnant. He would not wipe them out as a nation completely. It is as if God had a love affair with his people and even when they deserted him, and were unfaithful, and disobedient, he found it hard to let them go. The great magician, Harry Houdini, had a lifelong love affair with his wife. He was always writing her little notes. They always began, "Dear Bess, You'll never know how much I love you." She said that, long after his death, she was still finding those notes — in the attic, in the office, in pockets, and under things. How like God! He could not forsake his people if there was even a glimmer of a chance of their returning to him. They had been warned over and over; again and again they had been exhorted to repent. No matter what kind of punishment he sent to them now, they would deserve it. They had sinned beyond all the limits of Divine compassion — but, *unbelievably,* his great promise came to them, "*If* you repent ... I'll restore the kingdom, the house of David will rule once more over Israel and you will feast on wine and fruit in the promised land." There is always more mercy in God than there is sin in us.

An athletically gifted eight-year-old boy was dominating his junior soccer match. Although the game was only half-finished, he had kicked four of his team's five goals. The other team had not scored at all. When the game was almost over, the boy maneuvered his way to the mouth of the goal and another certain goal. But to the amazement of everyone, he just gave the ball a very weak tap, and didn't score. When the game was over, the boy's father said to his son, "Why did you do that? You could easily have scored another goal." "But, Dad," said the boy bleakly, "their goalie was *crying!*" God's great heart always goes out to his wayward children, and our tears of repentance move him to promise us forgiveness and restoration. God warns and entreats, and sure doom is foretold and judgment will fall, *but if we repent*, he will restore. Such a wondrous promise ought to make us fall deeply in love with the One who cares so much for us.

A remarkable lady named Minnie Pearce had the lead in the senior play during her college days. She worked hard on the part, and after the performance she was startled when a strange man came up to her backstage and introduced himself as the author of the play. He said, "I just wanted to come back and tell you that I have seen this drama many times, but tonight you embodied what I envisioned for the heroine better than anyone else ever has. Tonight, you made a dream of mine come true; you gave my play flesh and blood and I want to thank you." We can only ask ourselves the question, "Wouldn't it be wonderful to get to the end of the drama of this life, and there to meet the Divine Author, and have him say, 'You made the dream I had for you come true! What I had in mind when I created you is exactly what you did with your life's days and nights!' "

We still have a chance to get it right: to repent, to obey, and to claim the promise of God. That is an *unbelievable promise*!

Lectionary Preaching
After Pentecost

The following index will aid the user of this book in matching the correct Sunday with the appropriate text during Pentecost. All texts in this book are from the series for Lesson One, Revised Common Lectionary. Lutheran and Roman Catholic designations indicate days comparable to Sundays on which Revised Common Lectionary Propers are used.

(Fixed dates do not pertain to Lutheran Lectionary)

Fixed Date Lectionaries *Revised Common and Roman Catholic*	Lutheran Lectionary *Lutheran*
The Day of Pentecost	The Day of Pentecost
The Holy Trinity	The Holy Trinity
May 29-June 4 — Proper 4, Ordinary Time 9	Pentecost 2
June 5-11 — Proper 5, Ordinary Time 10	Pentecost 3
June 12-18 — Proper 6, Ordinary Time 11	Pentecost 4
June 19-25 — Proper 7, Ordinary Time 12	Pentecost 5
June 26-July 2 — Proper 8, Ordinary Time 13	Pentecost 6
July 3-9 — Proper 9, Ordinary Time 14	Pentecost 7
July 10-16 — Proper 10, Ordinary Time 15	Pentecost 8
July 17-23 — Proper 11, Ordinary Time 16	Pentecost 9
July 24-30 — Proper 12, Ordinary Time 17	Pentecost 10
July 31-Aug. 6 — Proper 13, Ordinary Time 18	Pentecost 11
Aug. 7-13 — Proper 14, Ordinary Time 19	Pentecost 12
Aug. 14-20 — Proper 15, Ordinary Time 20	Pentecost 13
Aug. 21-27 — Proper 16, Ordinary Time 21	Pentecost 14
Aug. 28-Sept. 3 — Proper 17, Ordinary Time 22	Pentecost 15
Sept. 4-10 — Proper 18, Ordinary Time 23	Pentecost 16
Sept. 11-17 — Proper 19, Ordinary Time 24	Pentecost 17

Sept. 18-24 — Proper 20, Ordinary Time 25	Pentecost 18
Sept. 25-Oct. 1 — Proper 21, Ordinary Time 26	Pentecost 19
Oct. 2-8 — Proper 22, Ordinary Time 27	Pentecost 20
Oct. 9-15 — Proper 23, Ordinary Time 28	Pentecost 21
Oct. 16-22 — Proper 24, Ordinary Time 29	Pentecost 22
Oct. 23-29 — Proper 25, Ordinary Time 30	Pentecost 23
Oct. 30-Nov. 5 — Proper 26, Ordinary Time 31	Pentecost 24
Nov. 6-12 — Proper 27, Ordinary Time 32	Pentecost 25
Nov. 13-19 — Proper 28, Ordinary Time 33	Pentecost 26 Pentecost 27
Nov. 20-26 — Christ the King	Christ the King

Reformation Day (or last Sunday in October) is October 31 (Revised Common, Lutheran)

All Saints' Day (or first Sunday in November) is November 1 (Revised Common, Lutheran, Roman Catholic)

92

Books In This Cycle C Series

Gospel Set

When It Is Dark Enough
Sermons For Advent, Christmas And Epiphany
Charles H. Bayer

Walking To ... Walking With ... Walking Through
Sermons For Lent And Easter
Glenn E. Ludwig

The Divine Advocacy
Sermons For Pentecost (First Third)
Maurice A. Fetty

Troubled Journey
Sermons For Pentecost (Middle Third)
John Lynch

Extraordinary Faith For Ordinary Time
Sermons For Pentecost (Last Third)
Larry Kalajainen

First Lesson Set

The Days Are Surely Coming
Sermons For Advent, Christmas And Epiphany
Robert A. Hausman

Turning Obstacles Into Opportunities
Sermons For Lent And Easter
Rodney Thomas Smothers

Grapes Of Wrath Or Grace?
Sermons For Pentecost (First Third)
Barbara Brokhoff

Summer Fruit
Sermons For Pentecost (Middle Third)
Richard L. Sheffield

Stepping Inside The Story
Sermons For Pentecost (Last Third)
Thomas G. Rogers

www.ingramcontent.com/pod-product-compliance
Lightning Source LLC
Chambersburg PA
CBHW070108070426
42448CB00038B/2124